2006 Poetry Competition

"I have a dream that my children will one day live in a nation where they will not be judged by the color of their skin, but by the content of their character."

Martin Luther King

I have a dream

words to change the world

- MOTIVATE your pupils to write and appreciate poetry.
- INSPIRE them to share their hopes and dreams for the future.
- BOOST awareness of your school's creative ability.
- WORK alongside the National Curriculum or the high level National Qualification Skills.
- Supports the *Every Child Matters - Make a Positive Contribution* outcome.
- Over £7,000 of great prizes for schools and pupils.

"When I was out there I was never ever alone, there was always a team of people behind me, in mind if not in body."
– Ellen MacArthur

Inspirations From Yorkshire
Edited by Gemma Hearn

 Young**Writers**

First published in Great Britain in 2006 by:
Young Writers
Remus House
Coltsfoot Drive
Peterborough
PE2 9JX
Telephone: 01733 890066
Website: www.youngwriters.co.uk

SB ISBN 1 84602 536 2

Foreword

Imagine a teenager's brain; a fertile yet fragile expanse teeming with ideas, aspirations, questions and emotions. Imagine a classroom full of racing minds, scratching pens writing an endless stream of ideas and thoughts . . .

. . . Imagine your words in print reaching a wider audience. Imagine that maybe, just maybe, your words can make a difference. Strike a chord. Touch a life. Change the world. Imagine no more . . .

'I Have a Dream' is a series of poetry collections written by 11 to 18-year-olds from schools and colleges across the UK and overseas. Pupils were invited to send us their poems using the theme 'I Have a Dream'. Selected entries range from dreams they've experienced to childhood fantasies of stardom and wealth, through inspirational poems of their dreams for a better future and of people who have influenced and inspired their lives.

The series is a snapshot of who and what inspires, influences and enthuses young adults of today. It shows an insight into their hopes, dreams and aspirations of the future and displays how their dreams are an escape from the pressures of today's modern life. Young Writers are proud to present this anthology, which is truly inspired and sure to be an inspiration to all who read it.

Contents

Sally Lindsay (13)	18
Emily Rowe (13)	19
Leanne Ward (12)	19
Rachel Glover (12)	20
Charlotte Marwood (18)	21
Faye Burton (14)	22
Stuart Goodsall (12)	22
Sarah Gibson (14)	22
Gareth Wheelhouse (14)	23
Ryan Nicholson (12)	23
Tom Sutcliffe (11)	23
Cheryse Wilson (12)	24
Michael Alloway (12)	24
Mark Paine (13)	25
Katie Lofthouse (12)	25
Tom Mills (14)	25
Jessica Hanslow (11)	26
Sarah Rutter (14)	26
Becky Gamble (13)	27
Anya Johnson (12)	27
Katie Adams (13)	28
Bex Gerrard (16)	29
Mathew Williams (12)	29
Rachel Scurr (13)	30
Michelle Telford (13)	30
Kelly McQuigg (13)	31
Emma Kirby (12)	31
Hannah Philipson (12)	32
Charlotte Featherstone (13)	32

King James' School, Knaresborough

Amy McMillan	33
Ellen Backhouse	34
Loz Minikin (13)	35
Chelsea Harris	36
Alistair Riddell (13)	37
Jack Bulmer	38
Becky Akroyd	38
Thomas Kelly	39
Cicily Wilkinson	39
Samantha Thompson (13)	40

Rossett High School, Harrogate

Robert Groom (13)	72
Alice Boothroyd (13)	72
Bethany Aitken (13)	73
Stacey Abendstern (13)	74
Alison Williams (13)	75
Emily Parker (12)	76
Josh Buckle (13)	76
Lauren Randall (13)	77
Ellie Murray (13)	77
Zahra Al-Moozany (13)	78
Catherine Payne (13)	79
Jenny Payne (13)	80
Rebecca Barnett (12)	81
Benji Robinson (12)	82
Jordan Mortimer (13)	82
Nikki Hall (12)	83
Amy Packham (13)	83
Emily Carse (13)	84
Ben Doyle (13)	85
Helen Jones (12)	86
Harriet Boyle (12)	86
Peter Hotchkiss (13)	87
Josie Fishkin (13)	87
Ben Bullock-Hughes (13)	88
Yasmin Pennock (13)	89

St Augustine's School, Scarborough

Claire Demmon (13)	89
Felicity Winkfield (12)	90
Emily Goddard (12)	90
Ben Stanyon (13)	91
Becky Rowley (12)	91
Jamie Banks (13)	92
Becca Harding (13)	92
Ruth Kitchen (13)	93
Jenny Mackenzie (13)	94
Poppy Smalley (12)	95
Amy Pearson (13)	96
Rachel Sharp (13)	97
Juliet Foote (13)	98

Settle Middle School, Settle
Madeline Crosswaite (12)   99

Skipton Girls' High School, Skipton
Sophie Devlin (12)   100

South Holderness Technology College, Preston
Jacob Wilkins (13)   100
Peter Reynolds (14)   101
Jessica Hitchcock (13)   102
Bekki Norrison (13)   102
Abbi Bainton (13)   103
Peter Richard Stones (18)   103
Katherine Brown (18)   104
Hannah Broadley (14)   105
Lewis Hodgson (14)   106
Matthew Copeman & George Christian (13)   107
Jessica Poole (14)   107
Danielle Agar (13) & Olivia Baker   108
Rebecca Crawley (13)   109
Laura Wattam (14)   110

Wingfield Comprehensive School, Rotherham
Thomas Baldwin (13)   110
Georgina Cutts (12)   111
Jade Reynolds (13)   111
Jake Phillips (12)   112
Jack Rowe (12)   112
Nicola Slazak (12)   113
Mitchel Wright (12)   113
Aaron Green (12)   114
Dale Goodwin (12)   114
Charlotte Harwood (13)   115
Paige Dow (12)   115
Waqar Majid (12)   116
Sinethemba Dumani (12)   116
Natasha Bell (12)   117
Danielle Jones (12)   117
Mariam Hassan (13)   118
Clarice Tejada (12)   118

Vicky Warrington (13)	119
Amy Gillott (12)	119
Rebekah Shortt (13)	120
Leigh-Anne Jones (12)	121
Laura Tompkins (11)	122
Marcus Senior (12)	123
Phoebe Trezise (12)	123
Jack Wright (12)	124
Harriet Cliff (12)	125
Robyn Brookes (11)	126
Chloe Bennett (12)	127
Madelaine Houghton (12)	128
Jamie Hensman (13)	128
Emma Woodland (12)	129
Adam Purshouse (11)	130
Ryan Bates (13)	131
Jade Dixon (11)	132
Kieran Bartholomew (12)	132
Bethany Cudworth (12)	133
Martin Harwood (13)	133
Nicola Howdle (12)	134
Luke Powell (13)	135
Rebekah Wilkinson (12)	136
Shannon Wheeler (13)	137
Phillip Pinder (13)	138
Kimberley Edwards (13)	139
William Burrows (13)	140
Sarah Coult (13)	141
Amy Adams (13)	142
Leanne Sanderson (11)	142
Lucy Brookes (13)	143
Chris Winsor (13)	144
Daniel Adams (12)	144
Tom Heap (12)	145
Ryan Broadhead (13)	146
William Humphries (13)	147
Judith Khumalo (12)	148
Elisabeth Kamaris (12)	149
Thomas Alderson (12)	150
Chloe Sanders (13)	151
Jade Haffner (12)	152
Jade Herbert (12)	153

The Poems

I Have A Dream

I magine world peace

H appiness for everyone
A lways tolerant
V ery understanding
E verlasting beauty

A ll sharing

D reams can come true
R espect others' differences
E verybody caring
A ll creatures live in harmony
M emories of love.

Alan Wade (16)
Applefields School (Special Needs), York

I Have A Dream

I believe in angels

H appy and playful
A lways there for you
V ery loving
E nter your mind

A nd give you peace

D irecting you to the right path
R eleasing pain and suffering
E nclosing their wings around you
A nd protecting you
M uch as they love you and the world!

Christopher Siggins (15)
Applefields School (Special Needs), York

A Wonderful Dream

I saw the snow going down from the sky.
I was dreaming about love and peace.
Between the people of the world.
No more wars all over the world.
I'm thinking about being nice to everyone.
I was dreaming about rainbows and happiness.
No more bullying to the other people.
Rainbows are beautiful, colourful and bright.
I'm thinking about bringing happiness to everyone.
I was dreaming about flowers.
No more being very naughty to the other people.
Flowers are colourful and lovely.
I'm thinking about the sun making a lovely sunny day.
I was dreaming about friendship.
No more calling names to the other people.
Make friends, be kind to the other people.
I'm thinking about being helpful to the other people.
I was dreaming about valour and freedom.
No more shouting and yelling to the other people.
Be brave to the other people of the world.
I see a bright star in the night sky.
I see two people getting married on a wedding day.

Laura Campbell (14)
Applefields School (Special Needs), York

This Futuristic Dream

A life with fear and bombs and shouts,
A life with storms and fogs and droughts,
A fearful world we couldn't live on,
We can change it together, if we work as one.

Now think about it carefully; what life should it be?
A life with happiness, where you live in safety,
Not a life with war where people fight and shout,
I guess that's a life that we can do without.

Where people live in peace and tranquillity,
That's the sort of life I think it should be,
Where people love each other, and children play,
On the seaside, in the autumn of the day.

What's the point of fighting, where lives will be lost?
They say 'It's to save our people', but at what cost?
The cost of lives, of course! The ones we're trying to save,
Even if those people are scoundrels, rogues or knaves.

My dream, this is, is for a better future.
A world with love and laughter, not pain and torture,
We will fall into fear, and death, it would seem,
If we don't follow this *futuristic dream.*

Mike Dutton (16)
Applefields School (Special Needs), York

I Have A Dream

I nclination

H armonies
A nimals live in peace
V oices of praise
E motional sadness

A dvocate of justice

D ance for joy
R ejoice for happiness
E nd of silence
A im to agree
M emories of love.

Afton Gemmell (15)
Applefields School (Special Needs), York

I Had A Dream . . .

I had a dream that the world was a better place,
Peace and love amongst the human race.
People to unite
And never fight.
Sister and brother
To love one another.
Bring peace and joy
To every girl and boy.
To stop all the wars and fights
And bring the world to perpetual love and light.

Daniel Edwards (16)
Applefields School (Special Needs), York

I Have A Dream

I mpressive

H omes for everyone
A bundance of food
V ision of peace
E scaping

A dulthood

D epression
R amadan
E migrated
A udience
M ascot

Rachael Robinson (15)
Applefields School (Special Needs), York

I Have A Dream

I mpressive beauty of nature

H omes for everyone
A bundance of peace
V isions of peace
E specially

A bove in the sky

D ance all around
R ainbow natures
E nd of wars
A ble to agree
M ake some friends.

Hannah Sawyer (15)
Applefields School (Special Needs), York

Party Peace

Listen up people
Stop the arguing
Stop the bombing
Stop the wars
And let's unite because you're invited to a party called Peace.
At Party Peace there is a better world.
People with different backgrounds and views are joining together
To create wonderful things, and are solving each other's problems
And combating life-threatening diseases and poverty.
Things like terrorism, racism and discrimination are a thing of
                                                    the past.

So come on down to the party.
You might enjoy yourself.

William Hodgson (15)
Applefields School (Special Needs), York

I Have A Dream

I wish people lived forever
Friends for everybody
Make everyone happy
Be nice to me
Have lots of fun
Play together
Share everything
Everybody be calm
Give to each other.

Lauren Farrow (15)
Applefields School (Special Needs), York

I Have A Dream

I nclusion

H appy
A ffection
V ariety
E quality

A ngels

D efend peace
R eally caring
E veryone to be friends
A helping hand
M arvellous.

Kayleigh Midwood
Applefields School (Special Needs), York

I Have A Dream

I have a dream that the wars
Will stop in Iraq
To make all the people
Have a better life
No more tsunamis
No more earthquakes
To make the people happy
In the whole world.

Matthew Theobald (14)
Applefields School (Special Needs), York

I Have A Dream

I wish for world friendship

H ope for world peace
A ll in the world
V alue
E veryone's life

A ngels

D eliver
R ejoicing
E veryone
A nd
M ake the world a better place.

Joshua Blackburn (16)
Applefields School (Special Needs), York

I Have A Dream

I deas

H ope
A ngels
V ariety
E mbracing

A ffection

D elicate
R ejoicing
E legant
A ngels
M agic.

James Fisher (15)
Applefields School (Special Needs), York

I Have A Dream

'I want to be a lawyer, Sir,'
I said to my teacher one day,
A dream of standing in front of the world
Fighting for your say.

'I want to be a lawyer, Miss,'
I'd seen it on TV,
I want to be involved in the world,
Not doing food, art or PE.

'I need to be a lawyer, Sir,'
I want the world to change,
From murder, abuse and stealing,
By people of every age.

'I need to be a lawyer, Miss,'
I could do so much,
No more murder, no more abuse . . .

Lauren Proudlock (13)
Carleton Community High School, Pontefract

My Dream

I have a dream that I can live in Las Vegas
With all the city life and crowds,
I wish that I could gamble
And join in all the fun,
I wish I could get the dearest house
With a pool, a gym and courts.
I wish I was a director
Working with all the stars.
I'd like to get real rich,
And be a movie legend,
All this is my dream,
I wish it would come true.

Luke Hall (12)
Carleton Community High School, Pontefract

I Have A Dream

I have a dream that it will never rain
That the snowflakes will fall and land on my nose.

I have a dream that no one is ever in pain,
That there are never any funerals.

I have a dream that bullying was never a word,
That no one had bad feelings, and everyone is heard.

I have a dream that everyone has a family,
That everyone is loved and cared for.

I have a dream that friends will stick together,
And divorces are just made up.

I have a dream that everyone will fit in,
And no one is all alone.

I have a dream that everything is cheap,
And that nobody says 'I can't afford this'.

I have a dream that birthdays can be enjoyed,
And that every day is enjoyed.

I have a dream that wishes will come true,
That happiness and love is forever and always.

I have a dream that the world will change,
That it will change into a better place.

Jessica Orchard (11)
Carleton Community High School, Pontefract

My Dreams

I have a dream that everyone will be loved,
I have a dream that the world can live in peace,
I have a dream that everyone will have a home,
I have a dream that no one will be poor,
I have a dream that no one will be the odd one out,
But the one main dream is that they all come true.

James Edwards (11)
Carleton Community High School, Pontefract

I Have A Dream

I have a dream that a bomb explodes
Blows a building high in the sky, guns sounding loudly.

I have a dream,
I'm a soldier,
A man shooting, throwing a grenade.

I have a dream riding on a truck
Taking a ride over the enemy lines.

I have a dream a bomb explodes, blows everything up apart from me
I'm the only one, there's no one else here,
I'm scared, I'm wounded and nearly dead.

I have a dream, I'm dying, just about to go
A man runs through the door, he shoots, I'm gone.

My eyes open, I'm alive, no I'm not, I'm in Heaven,
In a bed, there's the man who shot me.
Wait, I'm falling, everything's reversing
I'm back on the floor with a dead man at my feet
My friend behind him stood tall
Stood high, he smiles, I smile back.

Cameron Novelle Yates (12)
Carleton Community High School, Pontefract

My Dream

I have a dream that one day
I will become a comedian like Lee Evans
And I don't want to be like any of the Year 11s.

I have a dream that one day I will be a football player.
But I don't want to be a bricklayer.

I have a dream that one day I will become an actor
Like Bob Hope off Emmerdale.
But I don't want to meet Vivian Hope.

Lewis Riley (11)
Carleton Community High School, Pontefract

I Have A Dream

I have a dream
To be a footballer
To score goals
And tackle Rooney
I have a dream.

I have a dream
To beat Man U
And score a hat-trick
To win 10-0
I have a dream.

I have a dream
To play along the likes of Healy and Hulse
And score a hat-trick each
And to tackle Alan Smith
I have a dream.

Daniel Ward (12)
Carleton Community High School, Pontefract

She Inspires Me

Mum,
She helped me
Before she went away.

Thank you,
I wish
I had the chance to say.

Mum,
I miss you
I wish you were still here.

Alice Carrington (11)
Carleton Community High School, Pontefract

My Inspiration!

I am inspired by Robbie Williams
He is a great singer,
Even though he used to take drugs
Which made him a bit of a minger
He wants a child
He would be a great dad as he is a bit wild
He used to be in Take That
But now he's left they all don't chat!
He is a great showman and if he can be
I can be
You'll see,
When I win an award for best singer
I'll thank him
For inspiring me!

Courtney Harling (12)
Carleton Community High School, Pontefract

I Have A Dream!

I have a dream
On the stage
Crowds cheering wildly,
Being mind blown by our music,
'Acidic Dragon,' they shout,
We're on stage with radical guitars,
The arena erupting with electrifying sound,
'Rok on!' we shout
Making the sign of Rok!
The whole band surrounded by flames!
I have a dream.

Richard Howell (11)
Carleton Community High School, Pontefract

My Dreams

I have a dream,
To be a horse rider
To glide through the air,
To win medals,
To collect trophies,
Just to be the best.

I have a dream
To be an actress
The best actress in town,
To walk down the red carpet,
To collect my Oscar,
Cameras flashing in my eyes
For then I wake up
For that is my dream.

I have a dream
To see all the animals
To roar like the tiger,
To be as quiet as a mouse.
For that is my dream
And if all this came true
I would be the happiest girl ever!

Rebecca Kelsey (11)
Carleton Community High School, Pontefract

My Dream

My dreams are . . .
To discover the first full set of tyrannosaurus
Or be in the rugby league
Maybe I'll be an artist
All these things are dreams
I could be a wrestler
Or a rock star
All these things I could achieve
I'll set my sights on far.

James Wilson (12)
Carleton Community High School, Pontefract

Life

Life is full of celebrations
Somersaults, lifts, airs and graces
Laughter, movement running around
But all that has changed.
War broke out, people died
Rapists, murderers, all survived.
Guns, knives, what's true to you?
Nobody knows it's something to do.
Why did the world become so harsh?
We all used to hide in the garden of marsh.
Stories, films, which makes us kill
No one wanted to hear their will.
Please stop, it's just not fair,
No one can stop, not even the mayor.
Poverty, hunger and maybe drought.
Please let's throw it all out.
Bullies, racists, should be gone,
Maybe just maybe one by one
Children crying and screaming at night
Everyone resorts to a punch and a fight.

Megan Purnell (12)
Carleton Community High School, Pontefract

A Dream

A dream is when you fall asleep
When everything is still and quiet
Relaxing movement and drifting away
Floating on the white candyfloss above
Or the calm water of a river
Flowing along in a cloudy mist
Walking along the desert
Swimming in the sea
A dream can take you anywhere
A place where you can fly away
Flying away in a dream.

Jessica Lockett (12)
Carleton Community High School, Pontefract

My Dreams

My first dream is to be a famous rugby player,
To score trys here and there,
Or maybe to be the captain of Hull FC,
Or either the chairman of England rugby team.

My second dream is to be a wrestler,
I was inspired by the Big Show,
And the best Rey Mysterio,
And of course the Monster Kane.

My third dream is to be a mad scientist,
To blow up the school,
Or maybe create the world's best drink,
Or create a heck of a lot of monsters and robots.

My final dream is to make a sequel to the movie King Kong,
And make it the best!

Sam Spofforth (11)
Carleton Community High School, Pontefract

I Have A Dream

I have a dream that everyone around the world
Will be happy and live in peace.
I have a dream that friends will stay friends and never break up.
That blue skies will stay blue,
That the sun will shine.
I have a dream that dreams will come true,
That wishes will bring happiness around the world.
That birthdays will be celebrated,
That anniversaries will last,
I have a dream that people will enjoy their relationships,
That education will be fun,
That bullying will be banned.

I have a dream!

Nicola Olbison (12)
Carleton Community High School, Pontefract

My Dream As An Actress

My dream is to be an actress
It's my only ambition
Just like my idol Jessica Alba
Being in films like 'Honey', 'Deep Sea'
And 'Fastastic 4' just like her.
Walking down the red carpet to collect my Oscar award.
For everyone would know who I am.
1, 2, 3 cameras flashing before my eyes
Flash!
I wake up.

Chloe Trevelyan (12)
Carleton Community High School, Pontefract

I Have A Dream - Words To Change The World

My dreams for the world are . . .
All illnesses will be curable,
For both humans and animals,
No wars, world at peace,
No grudges over personal detail,
Everyone loved and cared for.

He has a dream
She has a dream
I have a dream too,
He has a dream
She has a dream
Dreams for the world too.

I have a dream that . . .
I would be able to travel the world
Reach my goals in life
Become a teacher
Have children
And live happily ever after.

Rebecca Leigh (13)
Harrogate High School, Harrogate

I Have A Dream

My dream is
To stop poverty,
Help the poor children through charity.

Bring everybody to peace
Have no more wars.

My dream is
To move abroad
To be known for helping
The sick and injured.

Stop crimes all around the world
Terrorists to stop and just live life

My dream is to see an equal world
For everybody
To have the same rights.

Shane Pope (13)
Harrogate High School, Harrogate

I Dream

I have a dream
A dream for life
To stop all wars
And save all life.

I also dream
The world could be
A happy one
With no split families.

I have a dream
A dream for me
To have a great future
And live in peace.

Sally Lindsay (13)
Harrogate High School, Harrogate

My Wonderful Dream

I can see a golden beach
Near the deep, blue, clear sea.

I hear the sea splashing
Against the rocky sharp cliffs.

I can smell the salty fish and chips
And the smell of fresh sugary doughnuts
That have just been cooked.

I can feel the nice, warm, clear sea
Against my sunburnt body.

I taste the cold, runny ice cream going
Down my throat.

I can touch the rough sharp starfish.

Emily Rowe (13)
Harrogate High School, Harrogate

My First Ever Dream

I can see a light blue swimming pool
With children running around it.

I hear children screaming and laughing
And I can hear the deep blue sea
Clashing against the grey rocks.

I can smell hot dogs coming from where the beach is
And I can smell the salt coming from the sea.

I can feel the warm air hitting my beige body
I can feel the cold water running through my fingers
From the swimming pool.

I can taste the salt from the sea.

I can feel cold water from the swimming pool.

Leanne Ward (12)
Harrogate High School, Harrogate

I Have A Dream!

I have a dream
Where everyone is glad
And nobody is sad.

I have a dream
Where hate turns to love,
Where the Devil is a dove.

I have a dream
Where sorrow turns to joy,
All children have a toy.

I have a dream
Where boredom turns to fun,
Where nobody has to run.

I have a dream
Where frowns turn to smiles,
Where nobody faces trials.

I have a dream
Of happiness and peace
For all the wars in the world to cease.

The world would be a better place
If all of this could be done!

Rachel Glover (12)
Harrogate High School, Harrogate

Better World

I have a dream
And in that dream
Lies a better world.

No more racism
No more sexism
No more inequality.

Everybody is given the same chances
The same choices
The same opportunity to make something of themselves.

Nobody is discriminated against
Nobody is looked down on because of their appearance
Nobody is belittled because of their background.

Everybody would hold respect for each other
Everybody would celebrate each other's culture
Everybody would accept each other no matter what creed,
Colour or race.

There would be an end to all war
An end to families being torn apart
And an end to devastation all over the world.

I have a dream
And in that dream
Lies a better world.

Charlotte Marwood (18)
Harrogate High School, Harrogate

My Dream Is . . .

My dream is to bring back all the good things
That have happened to me
To have my dad back so I can see him.

My dream is to go on holiday
Where I really like to go, Spain.

My dream is to be better at being good
With my mum and family.

My dream is to be happy with my family.

Faye Burton (14)
Harrogate High School, Harrogate

Stuart

S tuart's dreams
T oday I want to be on the tour
U p in the tour events
A t Tiger Woods' house
R iding the world's fastest buggy
T oday I'll be a champion.

Stuart Goodsall (12)
Harrogate High School, Harrogate

I Have A Dream

I have a dream that when I grow older
I will be a multimillionaire,
I want to marry a rich toy boy
I want to adopt little children
Who don't have a mum and dad.
I will help make peace.

    I want to do well.

Sarah Gibson (14)
Harrogate High School, Harrogate

I Have A Dream

My dream is when I'm older
That poverty will stop.
The world will be a better place
With everyone on top.
There will be no more bullying
Or fighting on the streets.
No more people starving
No more waifs and strays.
All the world just living
As they should day by day.
Pollution will be a thing of the past
We will all breathe the same fresh air.
For everyone deserves the same
No matter when or where.

Gareth Wheelhouse (14)
Harrogate High School, Harrogate

Chocolate

I wish there were chocolate pools everywhere
I dream that my house is chocolate
I hope I have three dogs
I want to live in a mansion
I really wish I was a rock star.

Ryan Nicholson (12)
Harrogate High School, Harrogate

Bikes

B ecome a Motocross rider
I would like to be the best Motocross rider
K it up my bike
E very day we go out on my bike
S oon have a CR125.

Tom Sutcliffe (11)
Harrogate High School, Harrogate

I Dream Of A World

I dream of a world
Where no one feels pain
Where poverty is stopped
And doesn't come back again.

I dream of a world
Where bears don't have to dance
Where they aren't made to leap
They aren't made to prance.

I dream of a world
Where lions aren't kept in cages
Made to suffer
So the keeper gets his wages.

I dream of a world
Where the ozone doesn't break
Tree-filled forests
And a pollution-free lake.

All these things are a part of my dream
From the mighty river
To the trickling stream.

One day I hope
That my dream will come true
So that life can be better
For me and for you.

Cheryse Wilson (12)
Harrogate High School, Harrogate

I Have A Dream

I have a dream

H oping that on Christmas
O f all the millions of people
P eople with wealth or poverty
E very single one will have another person.

Michael Alloway (12)
Harrogate High School, Harrogate

I Have A Dream

I have a dream
That all illnesses have a cure
That people live longer
That I am in the England cricket squad
I wish that everyone got on with each other
And there were never anymore wars.
        I really wish this would happen.

Mark Paine (13)
Harrogate High School, Harrogate

Dreaming

I have a dream,
Funny it seems,
To be a famous actress,
To be remembered,
By my fans,
For being different,
To others.

Katie Lofthouse (12)
Harrogate High School, Harrogate

I Had A Dream

I had a dream of the end of all wars,
Cotton candy, windows and chocolate doors.
Then I travelled across the world,
And the meaning of life unfurled.
I want to get the best car ever,
And get a couch made of leather.
Most of all I want my family to be rich
So I can get my own football pitch.

Tom Mills (14)
Harrogate High School, Harrogate

I Have A Dream

I have a dream
I have a dream
That I can have a dolphin.

I have a dream
I have a dream
To have a house of chocolate.

I have a dream
I have a dream
I can own the biggest shop.

I have a dream
I have a dream
To be a millionaire.

I wish I could
I wish I could.

Jessica Hanslow (11)
Harrogate High School, Harrogate

A Changed World

I have a dream,
That the world could change,
No murders, pain, illness or rape,
People suffer, people get hurt,
People live in fear,
Some people have no home,
No family, not even friends,
Not everyone is lucky,
Not everyone is happy,
Not everyone has money,
Put yourself in their shoes,
Help those people,
To not live in fear,
Change the world,
Change their lives.

Sarah Rutter (14)
Harrogate High School, Harrogate

Dream

I have a dream
A dream to be rich
A dream to be free
A dream to be me.

I have a dream
A dream to be
In a world with no wars
A dream with no split families
A dream to die peacefully.

I have a dream
A dream to stop poverty
A dream to never pay taxes
A dream to save lives.

Becky Gamble (13)
Harrogate High School, Harrogate

I Have A Dream

I have a dream
That no one shall be mean
Everyone is treated the same
No one shall go through pain
People will go through grief
But soon they shall have their relief
There shall be no more wars
But some more good laws
Every child shall have their knowledge
And soon hopefully go to college
No human shall be hurt
And certainly not treated like dirt
So I hope my dream is good enough
For everyone on planet Earth.

Anya Johnson (12)
Harrogate High School, Harrogate

I Want To Fly To Africa

I have a dream
To do something
That not many have done before
I want to fly to Africa
To help the needy and poor
One waterpump could save many lives
Lives that could have been lost
Lives of people any shape or size.

I have a dream
To do something
That not many have done before
One hospital
For a few small pounds
Could save more and more.

I have a dream
To do something
That not many have done before
One small animal
Could feed a hundred
A hundred for a hundred days.

I have a dream
To do something
That not many have done before
I want to fly to Africa
To help the needy and poor.

Katie Adams (13)
Harrogate High School, Harrogate

Dream To Be Free

I sit in my fortress,
Watching with pity,
The sugar-filtered screen,
Portrays them full of hope
Lessness is all they really have,
I feel I should help,
To clear my conscience,
But this barrier stops me,
Invisible though it is,
Like the screen they are on,
And I can feel better for,
Giving my two pounds to save a whole nation,
Of God's creation,
Their only dream to be saved,
And not be abandoned by their maker,
Standing in their masses with not a drop of water,
As I throw away food and tip my drink down
The sink, the dream here,
To be free from invisible barriers.

Bex Gerrard (16)
Harrogate High School, Harrogate

I Have A Dream

I have a dream
A dream that everyone in the world can play cricket and other
International sports together.
I have a dream where there are no such things as drugs.
Where there is a cure for cancer.
To have a world free of terrorism.
I have a dream that one day
I can play cricket for Yorkshire and England.

Mathew Williams (12)
Harrogate High School, Harrogate

I Have A Dream Words That Changed The World

I have a dream
Cars will be banned.
There will only be trains, planes, bikes.
Everyone will own a bike.
Everyone will be nice to each other.
No matter what race, religion or hair colour.
Lots of laughter.
Sad people will be sent to entertainment villas.
Their worries will be written down and thrown away.
Professional entertainers will make the sad laugh.
The world will be at peace.
No war, poverty, pollution, hunger and disease.
Everyone enjoying life!
Everyone happy!

Rachel Scurr (13)
Harrogate High School, Harrogate

Summer Wishes

On the first day of summer my wishes made world peace.
On the second day of summer my wishes gave money to charity.
On the third day of summer my wishes made everyone equal.
On the fourth day of summer my wishes got rid of poverty.
On the fifth day of summer my wishes saved the ozone layer.
On the sixth day of summer my wishes fed everyone in Africa.
On the seventh day of summer my wishes freed everyone
                                            from slavery.
On the eighth day of summer my wishes freed everyone innocent
                                            from jail.
On the ninth day of summer my wishes gave everyone a
                                            second chance.
On the tenth day of summer my wishes helped those who suffered.

    Don't just sit there . . . do something to help!

Michelle Telford (13)
Harrogate High School, Harrogate

Joy, Love And Happiness

I wish the world was full of joy,
That everyone got on,
Even people of different colour
That all hatred was gone.

I wish the world was full of love
That it flowed throughout the lands,
Africa, England, America too,
That we were part of each other's plans.

I wish the world was full of happiness,
That laughter was always around,
With adults, teens and children too,
No matter where you were, it could be found.

Kelly McQuigg (13)
Harrogate High School, Harrogate

I Have A Dream

I have a dream

H appiness and love all around the world
A ccepting people from every race
V ision of the future
E ducation should be a part of everyone's life

A bolish poverty

D eclaring war against each other, is it worth it?
R eligious discrimination has to stop
E rase pain from our lives
A mbitions and hopes
M aking a difference.

Emma Kirby (12)
Harrogate High School, Harrogate

Everyone

Everyone's ambitions
Deserve to come true,
With no conditions
Whatever they do.

Everyone should be treated the same
As each other,
Even if it houses pain
Whatever their front cover.

Everyone should
Be happy,
And should
No longer be snappy.

You can make a difference
For the better.

Hannah Philipson (12)
Harrogate High School, Harrogate

Wish World

I wish that there would be a world of peace
There would be no cruel, cruel beasts
Smoking would cease forever
Children would have the best time ever
Then people would live forever and ever.

I wish that there would be a world of richness
Everybody would be equal
And have as much happiness as and be clever.

I wish that I could travel the world
See all the people that are new
Go to lands no one has been to.

Charlotte Featherstone (13)
Harrogate High School, Harrogate

It's A Bit Shady!

Just lose it
When I'm gone
Eminem's my role model.

He started rapping for his baby girl,
When he split up with Kim,
Eminem's my role model.

In one way I felt sorry for him,
All on his own with little Hayley,
Eminem's my role model.

But his songs were always good,
He rapped about anything he could,
Eminem's my role model.

He lost everything even his family,
I'm cleaning out my closet,
Eminem's my role model.

He said, 'I'm sorry, Mama, I never meant to hurt you
I never meant to make you cry.'
Eminem's my role model.

The thing that is the best about Eminem
Is that he isn't afraid to stand up for what he thinks is right,
Eminem's my role model.

Eminem stands out from the crowd,
It shows that in 8 Mile,
Eminem's my role model.

But what is better than the best about Eminem,
Is that he isn't a coward, he is brave,
Brave to stand up for what he believes in,
Eminem's my role model.

Amy McMillan
King James' School, Knaresborough

My Mum

My mum is a star
She came from afar
She is thirty-nine
But doesn't drink wine.

As babies cry
Mums have tears in their eyes
She is a midwife
And brings in new life.

With brown eyes and glasses
She takes parent craft classes
She reads lots of books
But we never get a look.

Kate is her name
She's sometimes a pain
Three kids she has
One girl, two lads.

My mum is my best friend
Though she drives me round the bend
She'll be proud of me forever
We'll always be together.

Ellen Backhouse
King James' School, Knaresborough

Black Or White

Black or white he didn't care,
He tried to make the world aware,
Of what his people were getting told,
He didn't care. He stood bold.

The racism he couldn't stand,
He didn't need to make a grand,
For Martin Luther made a speech,
'I have a dream . . . ' and so he started to teach.

All he wanted was equal rights,
Some people said blacks were terrible sights,
Black's only the colour of their skin,
The colour is not thick, it's only thin.

After his speech he did not survive,
For someone didn't care, they shot him alive,
This sniper who shot him, the terrible beast,
He killed a great man, whose life is now ceased.

So there came an end to a wonderful man
He tried to stop racism, he showed one man can,
Martin Luther that was his name,
Stopping racism, that was his game.

Loz Minikin (13)
King James' School, Knaresborough

Daddy!

I love my dad,
He is the best,
He is always on his feet,
He never has a rest!

I love my dad,
He is so brave,
He always stays strong
When we go to my mum's grave.

I love my dad,
He is so cool,
Even though,
He beats me at pool!

I love my dad,
And the times we have had,
Have been amazing,
But also sad.

I love my dad,
I'm his little princess,
He always says,
He couldn't love me any less!

I love my dad,
Lots and lots,
I love my dad,
Like jelly tots!

Chelsea Harris
King James' School, Knaresborough

The Original Goon

No one today would ever match,
The original goon, the original catch,
Born in India in 1918,
Was the greatest comic genius the world has ever seen.

From the radio he went to TV
Writing scripts for channels like ITV
But the BBC was his real home,
Writing poems that became very well known.

He did many memorable shows,
Even in his life's highs and lows,
And even the Prince of Wales said,
'The day he's forgotten is the day I'm dead!'

Monty Python's Flying Circus,
Used many of his great ideas,
Until his nervous breakdown,
Which reduced him to tears.

After a well deserved rest,
He came back still the best,
Still amusing, still amazing,
The world of comedy never changing.

But at the age of 83,
He died of a belt of liver disease,
But his memory will still live on,
The comedy great, the number one . . .

Alistair Riddell (13)
King James' School, Knaresborough

My Inventors

Mummy and Daddy
They make me happy
They help the world as much as they can
That's what makes my daddy a man.
When I was a baby
They named me J B
They gave me a life
And I'm sharper than a knife.

My dad works hard
But eats a lot of lard
He drives me to football
And up the wall.
He's very nice
And as cool as ice.

My mummy
Isn't funny
But still very kind.
When she uses her mind
She's small
And very cool.

Jack Bulmer
King James' School, Knaresborough

Mum

My mum has given other children a home
And stopped them feeling alone.
Sometimes she felt let down, but kept on going,
Putting out her candle would take a lot of blowing.

She's supported me and my brother
My mum understands, I want no other.
She listens to my problems, and helps me out
And puts me right when I'm in doubt.

She's the backbone of our family
Without her I don't know where we'd be.

Becky Akroyd
King James' School, Knaresborough

Whatever, Never Mind

Drunken rock star.
Definite fighter.
Kurt Cobain was a mess!

He fought against his wife.
He fought against his life.
One day came a sad end for Kurt.

'I find it hard, it's hard to find the will whatever
Never mind.'

One day he got a shotgun.
And put it to his head.
Next thing the world knew Kurt Cobain was dead!

Don't be like me.
Don't lose hope like me.
Don't give up like me.

Thomas Kelly
King James' School, Knaresborough

Black And White

I have a dream to have a happy world as I am Martin Luther King.
I have a dream to stop racism around the world between black and
white people.
I have a dream that both black and white people have equal rights.
I have a dream that there is peace around the world and
Happiness throughout the people.

I have a dream that poor people are treated just like the rich
I have a dream that every person has enough food for the
rest of their lives.

I have a dream that I will fight for freedom for my people.
I have a dream that I will risk my life for others.
I have a dream that I will fight to save others because of racism.

Cicily Wilkinson
King James' School, Knaresborough

No Usual Woman

There is an English woman, who has gone and shocked us all,
Getting up, making it throughout every downfall,
Constantly going, carrying on no matter what,
Racing thousands, winning, beating the lot.

This is no usual woman, her strength's unbeatable,
Never before has a woman in her situation been so dutiful.

The respect she's gained by many is very well deserved,
Her enthusiasm alone makes many alike unnerved,
By the doctor's evaluation she's not the healthiest woman alive,
Yet nobody could call her weak as much as anyone could
call me Clive.

This is no usual woman, her strength's unbeatable,
Never before has a woman in her situation been so dutiful.

The woman I'm talking about has shocking nerves of steel,
The way she's pushed herself to the limit would make anyone
squirm and squeal,
Yet this amazing lady has never complained or groaned,
What she's put herself through, inspiring others,
She now has a gang
Jane Tomlinson's cloned.

This is no usual woman, her strength's unbeatable,
Never before has a woman in her situation been so dutiful.

When Jane was diagnosed with breast cancer, she did not cry,
She did not fear,
She simply decided to make the best of it, and she made that clear,
She ran for charity, Cancer research at that,
Although breathless, she ran, even with that lung tumour growing
large and fat.

This is no usual woman, her strength's unbeatable,
Never before has a woman in her situation been so dutiful.

Now Jane just keeps on running and cycling to the very end,
By the end I mean till she's finished, never will she give it up until
She's past the bend,
But even if she pulls out now, we'd think none the less,
Because Jane Tomlinson, our idol, comes from the very best.

Samantha Thompson (13)
King James' School, Knaresborough

Do They Know It's Christmas?

I got all of the singers and all of the bands
Showed them my anger, now we had some plans
We wrote a song, played it to the people
But do they know it's Christmas?

We did what it took to produce a song
Because in Africa so much was wrong
Gave all the profits to the starving millions
But do they know it's Christmas?

The song was a hit, it was played and played
TV made it huge, the famous Live Aid
A concert for the poor, the lost, the helpless
But do they know it's Christmas?

So citizens from every wealthy nation
Had wept over scenes of mass destruction
Next we strived to make governments listen
But do they know it's Christmas?

To end world poverty was Live 8's aim
And save all humanity from terrible pain
We've won the battle but not the war
And now they know it's Christmas!

Charles Green
King James' School, Knaresborough

Fly Like A Butterfly, Sting Like A Bee

Ali was as good in the ring,
As he was at helping people,
Although he was a heavyweight,
He was a softweight for the world.

He got the award for his deeds,
For helping those in need,
He inspired us all,
In and out of the ring,
He gave us all that special ping.

He was as popular as God,
For all his special things,
He helped the poor,
They lived in war.

One day to remember,
Must be the 15th of September,
When he got his award for his great deeds,
It was one of his best rewards.

This man was a gift from God,
A messenger of peace.

Tom Wills
King James' School, Knaresborough

Animal Hero, Steve Irwin

Steve Irwin was born in 1962,
He is the owner of Australia Zoo.

He's saved crocs, spiders and snakes,
Saviour every moment he wakes.

Lives with his wife and dog Bess,
To him they are the best.

He has done loads of documentaries
One of which is 'Dangerous Africans'.

He always says, 'Crikey',
And, 'Ain't she a beauty?'

Steve's dog died in 2004
They had fun with Sui before.

His parents Bob and Lyn,
Will always love Steve Irwin.

And that is the Crocodile Hunter,
For all we know he does utter.

Daniel McCormack (12)
King James' School, Knaresborough

My Role Model

My role model is my old grandpa,
Cos he's travelled the world so far,
Last year he took a trip to China,
He said that nothing could be finer.

He likes to play his games of golf,
He's been to tea with the Queen,
He's written some books on Meanwood,
And to 46 strange countries he's been.

In his shiny and glossy, green canoe,
He often paddles round the bay,
He never often catches much,
But he still dreams of the day.

He really enjoys his gardening,
But all he ever seems to grow,
Is lots and lots of green marrows,
And the occasional red tomato.

He's trekked through humid jungles,
Like the one in Papa New Guinea,
He's hoping to buy a new car,
Let's hope it's a bright pink mini.

He loves to take lots of photos,
It's just one of the things he does,
He's taken lots of pictures of landscapes,
And hundreds and hundreds of us.

He's my role model
He's my old grandpa,
He's been to many countries,
And he's travelled so, so far.

Fiona Bewell (12)
King James' School, Knaresborough

The Mercury Man

He was the life and soul of song,
The rock prophet, the *chosen one*
He was the sun, the sand, the sea,
His name was Freddie Mercury.

Freddie raved and rocked and rolled,
And ran and raced and remade souls!
He bipped and bopped and oohed and aahed
And strummed the strings of his guitar!

'Bismilla!' one day he cried, 'Oh Lord!'
'The world is sick and dead and bored!
I need a plan; I need a plot
To give the Earth, just all I've got!'

And so it was, that very night,
Freddie and his friends took flight,
They raved away from night till morn,
Until the mighty Queen was born!

The world began to shine that day,
Queen sang and sang to cleanse the bays!
The poor survived on their Live Aid Act:
Queen fed the Earth, and that's a fact!

But all their happy songs have ended
And Freddie sadly can't be mended
He's gone: the Lord of Death has spoken
And tears still fall, and souls are broken.

But don't despair my friend, don't fret,
This story isn't over yet!
It must be said, it must be told,
There's still some Freddie in us all.

Hannah Bruce (12)
King James' School, Knaresborough

The Heroes Of My Life

I have three mums
And they're my chums
There's one called Dawn
I'm so glad she was born
And she adopted me
Because my dad had to flee
I hate him so much
He used to be butch.

He tried to kidnap me
And who knows what I'd be
Andrea's also a stepmum
And she's no way dumb
And she was the first
But she was also a nurse.

We all love her
And like no other
And she will not leave
That she won't achieve.

But if so we'll be sad
And it'll be worse than bad
I also have a mum called Jean
And she is not at all mean
Plus she's very clean
And for that she's very clean.

When she knew I was almost kidnapped
Then she almost snapped
But she was also sad
And also she was half mad.

Adam Bateson
King James' School, Knaresborough

The Life-Changing Man

He was born in 1845,
And grew up to be an amazing man,
A life-changer . . . a money-raiser,
His words were, 'I'll do everything I can.'

Barnardo is who I'm talking about,
Thomas Barnado was his name,
He was a friendly, kind, caring man,
Saving poor children was his game.

He gave poor children a family,
And a home to live in,
He was determined to help all those kids,
Some of those kids lived in a bin.

Before he died in 1905,
He started Barnado support,
Some of the children he had helped,
Lived in the homes that he bought.

His dream was to help poor kids,
And of course his dream came true,
He was ever so pleased and joyful,
That he made children's lives happy not blue.

He gave them a cure,
For those who were dying,
And a shoulder to lean on,
For those who were crying.

When he died,
He had done everything that he could do,
He had tried his best, and worked really hard,
And now of course his dream has come true.

Georgia Sands
King James' School, Knaresborough

Always Has, Always Will

My best friend is tall and blonde,
And it's her courage that I am fond
She's totally cool and always nice,
Even though she's afraid of mice.

She always stands out in a crowd,
And is open, loud and proud,
But it's only me, her greatest chum,
That's known her since she was small and young.

It was when I was crouched down like a mouse,
At the playgroup, in the big brown house,
She yelled, 'Fire' as part of our game,
I tripped over - that was really lame!

But even though I hurt my knee,
So much so I was late to tea,
She stayed by my side till I stopped crying,
And assured me that I wasn't dying.

That was when we were only three,
We were young, we were free,
Ever since then she's been my mate,
The time we've had, it has been great.

Even when we were getting older,
To cry on there's always been a shoulder,
She's held me up when I was down,
When we've travelled round from town to town.

When moved from Aspin to King James,
We started playing different games,
Boys started coming on the scene,
The year we both turned thirteen.

Even though we've had our downs and ups
She'll always be my mate, right until we're grown-ups!

Lynette Pickering (13)
King James' School, Knaresborough

Someone Special

Everyone has someone special,
Dead or alive.

Someone who guides you along the way,
Holds your hand and reassures you
That everything will turn out right in the end.

I have someone special,
A friend.

They calm me when I'm frightened,
And we beat off the darkness together,
Side by side.

They have someone special,
A family.

A family that was never fully there,
A family that they had to gain piece by piece,
Until it was a real family.

But then they lost half,
The half they fought to keep,
They lost.

Everyone has someone special,
A role model.

Someone you look up to
And wish you were just like.

I have a role model,
When the darkness tried to kick them down,
They got back up.
When it took away the light,
They searched for a new one.
They never let the darkness bring them down.

I have someone special,
Do you?

Elisha Ainsley
King James' School, Knaresborough

My Flame

My mum is me,
I am her,
When she's with me,
I have no fear.
Many days come to pass,
She's still with me,
A true, strong, Yorkshire lass,
Many nights go by,
I shed my tears,
She's still here to fight my fears.

She's the light in the dark,
I'm the wood and she's the spark,
We're the fire burning bright,
The flame keeps rolling all through night.
The snow falls upon the fire,
It melts,
We're so strong forever,
Through any of the painful weather,
The flame still burns, strong together.

Nothing else to say,
No need to speak,
Without my mum I am weak,
As I grow, up and up,
She watches me with pride and love,
Life is this,
A realistic game,
Me and my mum,
My only flame!

Sasha Buck
King James' School, Knaresborough

She's A Champion!

For England she's won,
She's won lots of medals,
This is because
She'll never give up,
She'll never give up the challenges she takes.

She trains quite hard,
As it is tough,
It's tough being a runner,
But she'll never give up,
She'll never give up for our country.

Who's this you say,
It's Kelly Holmes of course,
The one person who got inspired for running,
When she watched the Olympic sports.

Today she's a star,
She's a star she is,
She runs like the wind,
I tell you she does.

I will tell you her dream,
Her dream today is,
To try to get children,
To be healthy and fit,
And to try to get children to eat fruit and veg.

But I'll tell you again,
She's a champion,
She is,
And I know that she'll never give up,
She'll never give up for the challenges she's faced.

Gemma Hewick (12)
King James' School, Knaresborough

Death, Disease, Now

Once upon a time upon this Earth
Good people starving and dying,
What people don't realise is that
Once upon a time is, now, too many people dying.

Some people trying to stop this, some people are trying to help
Bono has seen it, Bono is one of them
He has helped this problem himself.

Africans dying from starvation,
Whilst we have mountains of food,
Songs of anger, death and frustration,
Clean water would lighten the mood.

1, 2 I have no shoes
3, 4 there is no door
5, 6 I have only sticks
7, 8 my death is late
9, 10 a child dies again.

I have heard the politicians saying that something will be done
But what has been done?
Nothing!
If we want to save these people's lives
We will have to do it ourselves
Our money is how these people survive
Without your help there would be no lives to save.

Stephanie Cave (12)
King James' School, Knaresborough

My Superman!

The person who inspires me most,
Is not big-headed, he does not boast.
He's the most important man in my life,
My most important woman is his wife.

He knows everything there is to know,
He has travelled the world from high to low
He passes his knowledge onto me,
So I know too and travel and see.

He laughs at me and calls me names,
But I laugh too, we're only playing games.
He gives me advice when I'm confused,
His words and advice he has used.

To pick me up when I am down,
I hope that he will always be around.
I could not stand him to leave me,
Like he used to when he was in the navy.

He helped this country to fight for a cause,
In the Royal Airforce he fought some wars.
For me, my mum and sister he works
Amazingly hard but we have no Mercs!

Money doesn't matter to him at all,
Just us being happy as he loves us all.
Is it a bird or a plane? No and I'm glad,
It's my very own superman, it is my dad!

Louisa Moull (13)
King James' School, Knaresborough

Why?

It is my dream, to save our beautiful world,
Our hopes for safety have hurled.
The crocs have been around for millions of years,
If we don't stop it's going to end in tears.
What did that swan ever do to you?
Did you really need to drown the duck too?
That light you left on has just lost you some time,
Our time left to live is starting to decline.
That fishing hook you left by the lake
It's just killed a magnificent drake.

They're melting, they're melting, the ice caps are melting,
All because in your car you went belting.
You love dogs I know you do,
So why did you kick that one by the zoo?
I like to make people laugh; it's a common fact,
But there is some seriousness behind my act.
I save animals and help our land,
You can too, just make a stand.

Freya Watson (12)
King James' School, Knaresborough

Black And White

I had a dream to defeat racism.
I'm black, they're all white.
I will stand up for the fight.

I had a dream to defeat racism.
I stood up to make the black free.
Stop them being slaves.

I had a dream to defeat racism.
I did it but it's still out on the streets.

I had a dream to defeat racism.
I was shot dead, the white left me on my deathbed.

Martin Luther King.

Sam Hewitt (11)
King James' School, Knaresborough

Keep On Running!

I have a dream to win gold medals,
To run across that finish line.
I have a dream that those medals are mine,
The precious metal around my neck,
Standing on that raised-up deck,
In the middle standing proud,
The entire crowd cheering loud.

I have a dream to win gold medals,
Sprinting on that racing track.
I keep looking behind me, back, back, back,
The other runners sprinting fast.
However, I am running past,
I see another athlete gaining on me,
I'm not sure how long there is left in metres, four or three.

I have a dream to win gold medals,
I am standing on that raised up deck,
With two gold medals around my sweating neck.
I crossed that magic finish line,
Those golden medals are mine.
I am in the middle standing high and proud,
The entire crowd are cheering loud.

I fulfilled my dream to win gold medals.

I have a new dream to help young children,
To assist them to fulfil their dreams,
To be in the Great British teams.
They run around the racing track,
They are the ones looking back.
They're standing on that raised up wooden deck,
With gold medals around their necks,
Standing high and proud,
I am the one cheering loud.

They have fulfilled their dreams like me.

Gabby Crawford (12)
King James' School, Knaresborough

The Inspirational Geldof

He is Bob Geldof,
He wants to free Africans of poverty,
And he's a fantastic persuader,
At least he is to me.

He has saved people's lives,
And he has helped to persuade the world leaders,
All of Africa needs his help,
And they need us.

He has produced massive concerts,
Such as Band Aid and Live 8,
He gathered stars of all kinds,
Just to sing one song but a great song they made.

His name is Bob Geldof,
He's 55 years old.
He doesn't care if you're fat or thin,
All he wants you to do is help him.

But even now they still need help,
They yelp and yelp in pain,
As all their muscles clench,
It goes on all down their veins.

So that's Bob Geldof,
The African saviour,
Carry on saving all the Africans,
With your encouraging behaviour.

Emily Norton
King James' School, Knaresborough

It's Terminal . . .

'It's terminal,' the doctors say,
'You may not live another day,'
The cancer will take my life away,
Nobody knows . . .

I decided to fight the cancer back,
And prepare myself for another attack,
Whatever does my body lack?
Nobody knows . . .

My first challenge was the Great North Run,
Training was hard under the blazing sun,
I've achieved this goal but still I'm not done,
Nobody knows . . .

I travelled around the world with my brother,
Went from Rome to Leeds like no other,
On my bike for my family and mother,
Nobody knows . . .

'Jane Tomlinson,' people would shout,
'We support you as you had no doubt,'
'You cycled everywhere, from mount to mount,'
Still nobody knows . . .

The money for charity is rolling in,
One million pounds in the tin,
An MBE - that's my win,
Now everybody knows.

Abi Johnson
King James' School, Knaresborough

Untitled

Kylie Minogue, you are never alone,
Born in Melbourne, in Australia,
Since 1968, she has shown,
Life can be great.

She started being an actress, at a very young age,
Starring in the 'Sullivan's' and 'Neighbours',
As the rays of a brand new day,
Shine upon her until 2005.

In 2005 she was taken ill,
With a deathly disease,
She is not faking,
Day after day.

She has written many songs like,
'Confide In Me', 'Spinning Around' and more
All sorts, they belong,
To the rich and poor.

Trying to hide it, trying to live life,
Acting like normal,
Like the end of a knife,
Poor Kylie.

Daisy McBride
King James' School, Knaresborough

Geldof The Great!

He came to Africa
One day
And fed the children
He saved so many lives.

'Feed the world'
Were his words
'Make poverty history'
Was his game.

To raise money for people in Africa
No more would be dead
He needs your help
To save the world.

The world will never
Be the same
He put together
Some famous concerts.

Band Aid and Live 8
Which raised
So much money
He fed over one thousand people.

Megan Hooson
King James' School, Knaresborough

Deeds Not Words

She had a dream,
A dream to help all women,
To let them vote.

She had a dream,
A dream to create a campaign,
To create the WSPU.

She was determined,
Determined to unite 2000 people
She succeeded and helped them all.

Emmeline Pankhurst,
Helped them all
'Deeds not words' was her motto.

In 1879 she married a man,
A Manchester lawyer,
Who wrote a tale of her life.

In 1912 she was arrested once a month,
In jail she went on a hunger strike,
Her idea was called the 'cat and mouse'.

In 1918 women over 30 years
Had the right to vote,
Emmeline had passed that goal.

In 1918 Emmeline died,
With 'Deeds not words'
On her grave.

The suffragettes continued to campaign,
Then later that year,
Women over 21 were entitled to vote.

She had a dream,
A dream to help all women,
Which let them vote.

Katie Houldershaw (12)
King James' School, Knaresborough

Martin Luther King

I have a dream not a sequel
For everyone to be equal
Everyone has civil rights
So we can finally see the lights.

I have a dream that starts with a march
Which is called the Washington march
We will go for civil rights
Not for the sights.

I have a dream to tell everyone
We started as slaves but have united as one
All we want is freedom
Not to go around as slaves while you're on your bum.

I have a dream for no war
Just for fair law
Everyone has civil rights
So we can finally see the lights.

Robert Heptonstall (12)
King James' School, Knaresborough

I Have A Dream

I have a dream of free will
I have a dream of love
I have a dream of fairness
Peaceful as a dove.

I have a dream of equal right
I have a dream of caring
I have a dream of friendship
Living, loving and sharing.

I dream, a dream of loving
Will soon come true
I hope people believe
I do, don't you?

Rose Moule (13)
Rossett High School, Harrogate

Do You Have A Dream?

Do you have a dream?
Do you have a wish?
That everyone is equal
That everyone is loved
No one will be down
No one will be upset
I have a dream
Don't you?

Do you have a dream?
Do you have a wish?
That every creature runs free,
That every seam of self hope runs wild,
No creature will starve,
No tears will be shed,
I have a dream
Don't you?

I know you have a dream
I know you have a wish
I put my dreams forward
And I share my wishes
Why don't you?

Corrin Hornsby-Shawe (12)
Rossett High School, Harrogate

I Have A Dream

I have a dream
That guns and war will go away and,
Racial abuse fades.
So people don't have to die for their country.
People should feel safe in their homes.
So make these dreams come true.

Gaby Baltazar (12)
Rossett High School, Harrogate

Black, White, Green, Blue

Sitting on your leather sofa watching your TV
Lying in your comfy bed fast asleep and dreaming,
I have a dream,
That one day everyone will be equal,
Either black, white, blue or green.
I have a dream that no one will go hungry,
Either man, woman, ant or cat,
But one person can't make a difference,
Not the big man in the White House,
Not even Mr Tony Blair sending troops to Iraq,
Not even caring if they don't come back,
He just sits in his parlour day after day
Not caring what goes on in
Iraq, Africa, Peru,
They won't make a difference,
So we need you!

Megan Davies (12)
Rossett High School, Harrogate

I Have A Dream

I have a dream
To get racism from the world
Black, white, red, yellow
Whatever colour we are all equal
More equal rights
Less racial war
More countries united
Less poor, starving countries
No more boundaries
Everyone together, united as one
No one treated differently for their beliefs
No one treated differently for their background
No one treated differently for their colour.

Dom Brown (12)
Rossett High School, Harrogate

A Dream Of Peace

Atrocious, unstoppable conflict rages across the world
The hellish fires of war creep from nation to nation, engulfing them
The awful sounds of bodies dropping, guns firing
The expendable puppets of war, dying and suffering
For money grabbing, power hungry politicians, sitting safe
You wonder how they sleep at night
Don't you dream this could all stop?

I have a dream for a sudden,
Beautiful and eternal lapse in conflict
I dream that peace could reign across the globe
I dream that some seemingly impossible power
Will stop this horror that troubles us all
I dream that enemies could embrace, become friends
That the guns would stop, the mutilated bodies that litter the
battlefields
Like demonic confetti could be collected
I dream that people could be happy and the gruesome horrors of war
are stopped.

If only everyone could clear their sight
The tragic mindless killing could stop
The nightmare that the men and women on the frontline endure
could end
If despair could turn to hope in a flash of brilliance
All that they want to do is go home
Why does this seem so impossible?

I have a dream that we can paralyse vicious wars forever
I dream that we can stop the abominable massacre
I dream we can awaken people, open their eyes to the harsh realities
of war
I dream the guns can be silenced, the death halted
I dream that malicious, mortal enemies can come together in surreal
harmony

I have a dream
Do you?

Joseph Hughes (13)
Rossett High School, Harrogate

Can We Not Help?

All countries should be united
Money should be no object for help
There is no such thing as 'It's too expensive'
As the smiles of the helped would pay back all the money spent
Can we not help?

They have no luxuries like you and me
Well unless you call a drop of water a luxury
That is all they have
Thousands die every day
Can we not help?

Diseases spread like wildfire
They are lucky to survive
And there's us, we may get a cold
But compare
Can we not help?

So how can you say we can't pay for help
Is it too much to pay for these poor souls
Lying there, dying
What use is saving money when we can help them?
Can we not help?

Adam Firth (13)
Rossett High School, Harrogate

I Have A Dream

Sitting there looking at the garden
Bird feeders swinging in the cold wind
Reading my favourite magazine
Just come in from the RSPB
Birds flying here, hares bouncing there
And me sitting all wrapped up warm
These are what he has inspired me to do
He is funny, witty, clever and small
He is passionate about the wildlife
He is from the goodies and he is called Bill Oddie.

James Boyle (13)
Rossett High School, Harrogate

I Had A Dream

I had a dream
That I was the same as the next person
No one was different, no one the same
And no one cared.

I had a dream
That my voice could be heard
All across the world, throughout the countries
And no one ignored me.

I had a dream
That everyone was equal
I could show people who I really am
And no one gave me funny looks.

I had a dream
That as one we stood up
And did what we wanted to do, together
And no one complained.

I had a dream
That we all got along . . .

Have you?

Laura Dallas (12)
Rossett High School, Harrogate

I Have A Dream

In my dream there is no suffering.
There is no poverty or drought.
Nobody has power over everyone,
And no one is given grief for their colour or creed.
There will be no tears shed unnecessarily,
And no war that puts innocent people at risk.
I have a dream,
But can dreams come true?

Sophie Corbett (12)
Rossett High School, Harrogate

I Have A Dream

As I sit there
Watching her win

I think *wow*
As I look at her grin

She smiles
As she wins to victory

The sound of cheer
Fills the air

Sitting there clapping
Wishing I could be there

Collecting the medal
In the bright yellow sun
Holding it up
Thinking that was fun

Watching her win
For England
With smiles all round

Shouting, screaming
Clapping
Everyone around laughing

Thinking what it
Would be like

Wishing I was there
Tonight.

Kelly Holmes
The Nation's favourite.

Elizabeth Bourke (13)
Rossett High School, Harrogate

I Have A Dream

I have a dream
To change the world forever
Why can't all fights and wars stop?
So we can have peace all around.

I have a dream
For racism to stop
So there'll be no discrimination in the world
And to let black and white be equal.

I have a dream
To let no one starve to death
And that everyone can have enough food to eat
So why can't there just be enough food to go around?

I have a dream
To try and stop fatal diseases from killing us
So why can't everyone drink fresh clean water
And everyone to be equal in the world?

I have a dream
To stop all suffering and poverty
So no one will die of starvation
And every country should become equal with each other.

I have a dream
To make the world equal and fair
And for everyone to be treated in the same way
Do you?

Rebecca Middleton (12)
Rossett High School, Harrogate

I Have A Dream

I have a dream
That people will judge us on our personality
Not our skin colour
I have a dream
That we will be able to walk down the street
With no racist comments shouted our way
I have a dream that one day, maybe just one day
Everything will be how it should be.

I have a dream
That we will be accepted wherever we go
Not only in certain places
I have a dream
That everywhere will be multicultured
Not just a few countries
I have a dream that one day, maybe just one day
Everything will be how it should be.

I have a dream
That racism will stop and
No more dirty looks will come our way
I have a dream
That we will not even notice people's skin colour
Because we are all the same
I have a dream that one day, maybe just one day
Everything will be how it should be.

Katie Burns (13)
Rossett High School, Harrogate

I Have A Dream

I have a dream
That may be a reality one day.
There will be no pain or suffering
No poverty or starvation
No war or fighting
No hate or racism.
But to live in a world
Where everyone has equal rights
Where everyone has enough food
A peaceful world, a fair world.
A lot of people will agree with me
So why do we continue to let this happen?
If everyone got together
We could put a stop to all this now.
End the pain and suffering
End the war and fighting
End the hate and racism
This fantasy world could be real
But it won't if we don't do a thing.
This is my dream.

Shona Whiteley (12)
Rossett High School, Harrogate

I Have A Dream

This is the time for me to say
Who I admire the most
She's brave
She's willing
She's daring
She's eager to follow her dream
I have a dream to become like her
I have a dream to be a champion
I have a dream to make a difference
I have a dream, a dream I want to follow.

The person I admire the most is Ellen MacArthur.

Hannah Staiano (13)
Rossett High School, Harrogate

This Is My Dream

I have a dream
To be the manager
Of the England football team
I want to coach them
To be the best
So they can beat all the the rest
Whoever it is Germany or France
They'd be so good
They'd have the best chance
I'd make them try
With all their might
So they would always win the fight
So that's my dream
And it will come true,
It will, it will, I bet you!

Raffi Jones (12)
Rossett High School, Harrogate

People Should Be . . .

People should be judged by who they are,
Not by race and colour.

People should be given equal opportunities,
Without being branded.

People should be treated all the same,
Without being judged by where they live.

People should be paid equally
Not by whether they are male or female.

People should be given benefit of doubt,
Without being judged by looks.

People should be who they are,
Not who they are told to be.

Megan Reeves (13)
Rossett High School, Harrogate

I Have A Dream For Freedom

I have a dream
Everyone can be even
People are getting beaten
Cos of their skin colour
Being murdered
Being slaughtered
Being starved to the bone.

I have a dream
Poverty will vanish
Cos people are famished
Livin' under the line
Which is just a sign
That no one gives a damn.

Freedom
Freedom for speech
Freedom for love
Freedom of their life
I would give people freedom
If I could just do it
This is my dream.

If only it was yours.

Robert Groom (13)
Rossett High School, Harrogate

I Dream

I dream that I will be remembered for the rest of time,
I dream that I will make a difference in the world,
I dream that I will forever shine,
I dream that I am the one and only,
I dream that there will be no other athlete like me,
I dream that I will set a world record,
I dream that I will be an athlete,
I do have a dream.

Alice Boothroyd (13)
Rossett High School, Harrogate

AKA Pako

Pako is a dance teacher
But not your average one
He has dance schools around the world
For just about anyone.

He started off in Portugal
13 and playing football
He swapped it for ballet one day
And took expected ridicule.

'You're gay, Pako,' teased his team
'Yes I suppose I am
Dancing around with 19 girls
'Stead of you lot, gay I am.'

He mastered ballet, jazz, hip hop
And then decided he would
Teach the world his new found skill
Until we were all as good.

He carried on until this day
And now he's 25
Teaching Denmark, Portugal and England
How to body pop and jive.

In spite of all his achievements
He's still as modest as can be
'Yeah - I'm an alright dancer
I'm the black dude, Pako, I'm just me.'

The morale to this story
Is be what you want to be
Anyone can do it
Including you and me.

It takes a lot of effort
But you'll do it in the end
Just remember what Pako did
My dancing black dude friend!

Bethany Aitken (13)
Rossett High School, Harrogate

I Have A Dream

I have a dream.
Tears falling down,
Just because they are different.
When will we be able to tell them,
Everything will be alright?
Those nightmares have turned to reality.

I have a dream.
That we wouldn't have to leave,
Those people crying in the dirty streets.
That we won't have to look at them,
Differently just because of their looks.
Why have those nightmares turned to reality?

I have a dream.
That everyone is equal.
Those people could go where they wanted,
Without being banned and told they can't.
What has happened to the world?
The nightmares have turned to reality.

I have a dream.
That those people will not,
Be treated horribly in slavery.
The sun could shine on them and they could be happy.
Stop racism now!
Because those nightmares have turned to reality.

Stacey Abendstern (13)
Rossett High School, Harrogate

I Have A Dream

I have a dream
It's not as impossible as it may seem.

Give me one good reason
Why all the fights and wars
End just for the festive season,
Does war really have a good cause?

I have a dream
It's not as impossible as it may seem.

'Let's kill each other'
'Let's start another war'
We should treat our neighbours like a brother,
But, power and money, people just want more.

I have a dream
It's not as impossible as it may seem

Poverty exists
Even in America and Britain
People still fight with guns or fists
That's why this poem was written
I have a dream
It's not as impossible as it may seem.

It does seem
I want equality like when the world was new,
I have a dream
Why can't it come true?

Alison Williams (13)
Rossett High School, Harrogate

I Have A Dream

Floating in a gentle sleep
Wondering what to be,
Should I sail across the deep,
The deep, open, blue sea?

No I want to write as well
As this woman can,
Exciting stories to read and tell,
She doesn't care about a tan.

Candyfloss and Lola Rose,
Tracy Beaker too,
She does not have flashy clothes,
But writing stories is what I will do!

I want to be just like her,
Like Jackie Wilson - of course,
Her head is not a big blur,
And is not filled with remorse.

I think Jackie is the best,
Because she writes better than the rest.

Emily Parker (12)
Rossett High School, Harrogate

I Had A Dream . . .

I had a dream that life one day
Was a million times better than it is today
When all bad things were washed away
Hate, terror, violence and murder,
But . . .
It was only a dream I had that day,
'Bout life being better than it is today.

Josh Buckle (13)
Rossett High School, Harrogate

She's A . . .

She's a chauffeur
And a purse
She's a psychiatric nurse.

She's a cleaner
And a cook
She's a walking, talking book.

She's a hug
And a kiss
She's a star you cannot miss.

She's a daughter
And a friend
Any problems she will mend.

She's always happy
Never glum
She is the world's best ever mum!

Lauren Randall (13)
Rossett High School, Harrogate

I Have A Dream

I have a dream to be like Darcy
A dancer with style and flexibility
I have a dream to dance
Where I can twirl and prance
I have a dream to act
Wow the audience with great impact
I have a dream to perform
Where I can feel free and reborn
I have a dream to do the highest leap
Higher than a mountain peak
I have a dream to be the best I can be
I dream to be like Darcy.

Ellie Murray (13)
Rossett High School, Harrogate

I Have A Dream

I have a dream
To stop world hunger
Following Geldof's ways
For families to be whole again
And have a meal a day
It's not your children's bones we see.
What must it be like,
Living a life filled with misfortune
Not knowing whether you will
Survive another day?
Families torn apart,
With the loss of another.
Their eyes portray their sadness
Can't we do anything to stop this?
Why don't we share their madness?
We sit here with our plates filled high
While their mothers beg for food
It's not as though they ask for much
Only your gratitude.
How can we see their weary faces
And feel no remorse?
I'd rather have the peace of mind,
Than any full course
They need to know they're not alone
That you are on their side
I have this dream
Don't you?

Zahra Al-Moozany (13)
Rossett High School, Harrogate

Life's A Bowl Of Dreams

I had a dream where the sky was full of pinks and yellows
And where everyone was happy little fellows.

I had a dream where children skipped and jived
And where penguins dipped and dived.

I had a dream where I was in a comedy show
And everyone's face had a happy glow.

I had a dream where I was a flower
And the entire world was in my power.

I had a dream where I was a rocket
But the plug wouldn't fit in the socket.

I had a dream where the caged animals roamed free
And they were all as cute but annoying as the buzzy bee.

I had a dream where the snow fell on the ground
And the footsteps didn't make a sound.

I had a dream where I was a red beating heart
But I was ravenously ripped apart.

I had a dream that Earth was a cup of tea
But somehow got chucked into the sea.

I had a dream where I was a book
But I wouldn't let anyone have a look.

I had a dream where life was a song
But then it ended with an almighty *gong.*

I had a dream that people acted fake
But then I realised I was awake.

Catherine Payne (13)
Rossett High School, Harrogate

Never Stop Reaching

Inspired me she did -
To think positive and strive
For the thing I want the most
Out of the world's surprises.
She told me a short story
About how she was put down -
She was told so harshly
That her favourite dream to be;
Was a total waste of wishes.
But this did not stop her
From trying oh so hard
To arrive at where she wished to be.
And there she was in front of me
Living out her dream!
Let this be some good advice
To never ever give up;
Keep reaching to your wish
No matter what some others say -
For are they you
Or are you them?
No! So just ignore them
This is what she taught me
And now I want to teach you,
Never let go of your dreams!
They will come to you -
My part-time teacher told me;
At primary school . . .

Jenny Payne (13)
Rossett High School, Harrogate

A Dream To Change The World

Each night she laid in bed
Getting not a wink of sleep
Because of all the gunshot sounds
That would never cease.

The music of the war time
She hated it a lot
She wished that clearly some day soon
It would all just stop.

She found she didn't need things
That she used to have
And that her most beloved things
Were family, mum and dad.

The black hole of her mind
Was full of misery and woe
She wished all war and gunshot sounds
Simply would just go.

She wished that she could make,
The badness go away
But she was too scared to tell someone
So war would have to stay.

The bad had overrun her
The days they seemed so long
But when she told the world her dream
She found that war was gone.

Rebecca Barnett (12)
Rossett High School, Harrogate

Animal Rights

I have a dream,
That animals are free,
As free as the human race.
Testing, killing for no apparent reason.
But why, why is this?
Who will save the monkey?
The lone dog that will die?
Who will finally stop it?
Who will stop the kitten from dying
Alone on the street?
Who will stop the bird from falling?
The fish from sinking?
The monkey slipping and dying?
Who will stop the hunting,
The shooting and the killing?
Who will save the tiger
And stop the king losing his thrown?

Benji Robinson (12)
Rossett High School, Harrogate

I Have A Dream

Steven Gerrard is the best
He really must be blessed
He makes driving runs through midfield,
To his goal he is a shield.

He plays in midfield with a bullet of a shot
When you blink the ball is a dot,
He really, really inspires me,
He works so hard for Liverpool FC.

More often than not he scores a goal
He plays with his heart and with his soul
He is so brilliant and always busy
That is why he inspires me.

Jordan Mortimer (13)
Rossett High School, Harrogate

Abraham Lincoln

Abraham Lincoln should inspire us all . . .

Born February 12, 1809,
Lived in Indiana in a cabin made of pine.

He struggled for a living and a good education,
Yet that did not stop him from running the nation.

Mary Todd Lincoln was his wife's whole name,
Then in 1860 the sixteenth president he became.

It was Good Friday - April 14, 1865 . . .
Later that evening he was no longer alive.

Assassinated, he was, by John Wilkes Booth,
This actor didn't like it when Abe told the truth.

Magnificent, magnanimous and mighty was that man,
Who's goal was to free slaves in their promised land.

Now the Lincoln Memorial is here to show,
In Washington DC for everyone to know.

Abraham Lincoln should inspire us all . . .

Nikki Hall (12)
Rossett High School, Harrogate

I Have A Dream

Kelly Holmes is who I admire,
She runs a race as fast as fire
She gets the crowd to cheer so loud
And makes all of England proud
She trained and trained in rain and cold
Until she won Olympic gold.

She inspires me to win the race
I would have a great smile on my face
And just like her, when things get rough
I will stand tall and be that tough.

Amy Packham (13)
Rossett High School, Harrogate

Nanny

She inspires me
She's no celeb
She's my family.

I love her with all my heart
She fills the world with love
She's sweeter than a creamy tart.

I share my problems with her
She listens to me
I know she's there.

She shares with me
Really good advice
We always sort it over tea.

She tells me to try my best
To try with all my might
She tells us to beat the rest.

The person who inspires me
Is very precious
This person is my nanny!

Emily Carse (13)
Rossett High School, Harrogate

I Have A Dream

I have a dream
A dream I can fly
In my rocket
I touch the sky
I fly with the clouds
Thirty thousand feet high
1000 miles fast
I want to try
To take my carrier
Higher, higher
To break the barrier
And touch the stars
In the vacuum of space
To see the planets
In a magical place
I see my prize
It's big, it's red,
It's mine, it's Mars
Onto the surface I tread
The ground is soft, untouched
My dream is coming true
Neil Armstrong
I did it for you.

Ben Doyle (13)
Rossett High School, Harrogate

Kelly Holmes

My idol is an inspiration
To every boy and girl
All across the nation
Let her talent unfurl.

She battled the tiredness and pain
Which ended in success
She then did it again
Which challenged her no less.

But she won that too
Which filled her with glee
And everyone knew
She was happy as could be.

She's a role model to me
Kelly Holmes - and will always be.

Helen Jones (12)
Rossett High School, Harrogate

My Father

I have a dream, to follow on,
Like this person, who's never gone.
A kind and gentle lively soul,
Who doesn't give up, and achieves his goals.

Whether for his music choice,
Rock and crazy screaming voice.
He gives me freedom, he gives me time,
To learn what is right, to educate my mind.

'Live and learn' my father says
'You'll never forget those days.
Whether you're right or very wrong
I'll always care for you so strong'.
My father, he inspires me
To live my life such as he.

Harriet Boyle (12)
Rossett High School, Harrogate

My Inspiration

Steven Gerrard, Liverpool Captain,
That's who inspires me,
He might only be one man,
But he does the work of three,
Ronaldinho's good as well,
Out of all he is the best,
His skills are where he excels,
I think he's simply blessed,
Thierry Henry, goal-scoring king,
The last of my heroes,
When he comes on the pitch the crowd shout and sing,
Just wait, a goal will follow,
These are the stars that inspire me,
In football they are top of the tree.

Peter Hotchkiss (13)
Rossett High School, Harrogate

I Have A Dream!

I have a dream to win the race,
I have a dream to be the best,
I have a dream to keep the pace,
I have a dream to take this test,
I have a dream to win the gold,
I have a dream to sprint so fast,
I have a dream to be that bold,
I have a dream to never come last,
I have a dream to really shine,
I have a dream to feel the pain,
I have a dream to step over the line,
I have a dream to break open champagne,
If that was me the world would be a blur,
I really want to be like her.

Kelly Holmes inspired me to write this poem.

Josie Fishkin (13)
Rossett High School, Harrogate

I Have A Dream

From great whites
To small mites
I have a dream to see them all
From huge whales
To slimy snails
I have a dream to see them all.

From stormy seas
To buzzing bees
I have a dream to see them all
From mountain high
To leopards shy
I have a dream to see them all.

From the bright colours of the macaw
To millipedes crawling across the floor
I have a dream to see them all
From horned goats
To cheeky stoats
I have a dream to see them all.

Like David Attenborough!

Ben Bullock-Hughes (13)
Rossett High School, Harrogate

I Have A Dream

Kelly Holmes
Big and bold,
Inspires me
With her Olympic gold.

All the time
She tries her best
Never will settle
For anything less.

She's a fighter,
She goes far,
She's determined
She's a star!

I like to think
That I could be
That good at something
She inspires me.

Yasmin Pennock (13)
Rossett High School, Harrogate

Night Journey

My bed is like an aeroplane,
When I'm tucked in nothing is the same.
I fly off to places far away
And leave behind my busy day.

I fly past oceans, turquoise blue,
Glide over places I never knew.
The palm trees wave to me on the shore,
Then . . . I see my bedroom floor.

I blink my eyes, I scratch my head,
The journey's ended, I'm back in bed.
My plane goes flying every night,
And glides back home in the morning light.

Claire Demmon (13)
St Augustine's School, Scarborough

Jungle Dream!

There's a tiger in the bedroom
And a monkey in the hall,
There's a massive boom,
Now there's a hole in the wall.

The giraffes are eating grass,
Elephants are cooling themselves with water,
The lake looks like glass,
My brother's talking to an alligator.

Snakes are slithering around the trees,
Zebras changing colour,
In the summer's breeze,
I'm sure I can see the Queen's mother.

Monkeys swinging above my head,
Rhinos stampeding down a stream,
Then I found myself in bed,
Only to find it was another dream.

Felicity Winkfield (12)
St Augustine's School, Scarborough

I Have A Dream!

I have a dream about a butterfly which flutters by
In the sky
And it sees everyone as equal
Everyone has a chance
And it sees everyone the same from England to France.
You could be happy or sad,
Be a girl or a lad,
Eyes be blue or brown,
Live in a city or town.
I have a dream about a butterfly which flutters by.

Emily Goddard (12)
St Augustine's School, Scarborough

My Dream

D reaming on a warm summer's day
R eading near the cool sparkling bay
E ating melted ice cream in the heat
A lmost asleep on a pillow of wheat
M y dream, my dream, my dream.

D ancing on the cool silver sand
R acing in the foamy white spray
E nticing my friends into the sea
A cross the waves in slow motion
M y dream, my dream, my dream.

D reaming of a holiday in the sun
R emembering places this dream began
E nriching my life with wondrous sights
A live to my dream that has begun
M y dream, my dream, my dream.

Ben Stanyon (13)
St Augustine's School, Scarborough

Dreams

Dreams are beautiful
Dreams are great
Dreams are sightful
Dreams, you never want to wake.

Dreams are peaceful
Dreams are excellent
Dreams are enticing
Though nightmares are exciting.

Becky Rowley (12)
St Augustine's School, Scarborough

A Dream In War

I have a dream as I sit here now,
A way to cheat death somehow.
So as I sit in the trenches filled with lice and mud,
Another shell hits, thud!

I have dreams while bullets fly,
A solemn wish before I die.
Peace between all men on Earth today,
To bring a ray of sunshine in this dark month of May.

As the gas cloud silently kills,
Soldiers look over the bloody hills.
Looking for a ray of hope,
I start to climb a muddy slope.

So think of us in times to come,
Bless our graves and the songs we hum.
We kill for caves just
But dream for the future, that we must.

Jamie Banks (13)
St Augustine's School, Scarborough

Tapestries In My Mind

Tapestries woven out of the finest wool,
Stories written in my mind,
Tales hidden inside my head,
Which only I can find.

Like the endless vacuum of space,
My dreams go on forever.
Allowing me to swim through deepest oceans,
Or fly as light as a feather.

Fantasy tales created in my mind
But when woken in the morning,
I see I cannot find,
The tapestries woven in my mind.

Becca Harding (13)
St Augustine's School, Scarborough

I Have A Dream

I have a dream of candyfloss clouds,
I have a dream of a marshmallow sky.
In my dream I spread my wings,
I have a dream that I can fly.

I sail above the clouds,
I drift towards the sun.
I soar over the treetops
Laughing, having fun.

I float through the air,
Spinning, twisting around
Everything's still and peaceful,
There isn't any sound.

A breeze lifts my hair,
The air is calm and cool.
I keep on sailing through the sky,
Feeling happiness through and through.

I'm flying faster now,
Travelling at the speed of light.
The wind whips through my body,
I'm dancing through the night.

I'm empowered, I'm flying free,
I'm soaring over the world.
Underneath me I can see,
Countries and oceans unfurled.

I wake up in bed that night,
The dream has vanished, it's gone.
But I know that one day I'll find my dream,
Because my dream is Heaven.

Ruth Kitchen (13)
St Augustine's School, Scarborough

I Have A Dream!

Snow drifting steadily
Children smiling cheerfully
Rain falls like a steady stream
I have a dream.

The sun shining in the sky
Butterflies fluttering by
Fresh strawberries and whipped cream
I have a dream.

Little lambs bleat in the field
A brave knight with sword and shield
All around me are light beams
I have a dream.

I can smell the sweet flowers
I have almighty power
And we are the winning team
I have a dream.

All of my visions have gone
I have no memory of one
They are all ripped at the seams
I have no dreams.

Jenny Mackenzie (13)
St Augustine's School, Scarborough

I Have A Dream

People crying,
People fighting,
People dying,
This shouldn't be.

I have a dream,

People dancing,
People singing,
People laughing,
People winning.

I have a dream,

People cheating,
People bombing,
People beating,
This shouldn't be.

People talking,
People smiling,
People walking,
Without a care in the world.

This is my dream.

Poppy Smalley (12)
St Augustine's School, Scarborough

My Nice Dream

I have a dream that everyone's equal,
Happy, cheerful, full of contentment.
Black children and white children will run round in a circle,
Knowing that world peace will be always around them.

No one is racist, abused or let down,
Everyone's happy, there's no need to frown.
No one's being bullied, kidnapped or raped,
Nobody hates others, we are all mates.

There are also no wars, only people shaking hands,
No one is smoking, drinking or in gangs.
Fear is forgotten and never took place,
Sleep on; sleep on the good human race.

I hope I'm not dreaming or Heaven is here,
Wake up to reality - full of good cheer.
Well rested and happy I get out of bed,
I can do anything, it's all in my head.

Amy Pearson (13)
St Augustine's School, Scarborough

Dreams

Dreams are cool
Dreams are funny
Dreams are clever
Dreams are yummy
Dreams are magic
Dreams are tragic.

I love dreams they
Make me tingle or
Take me to places
I've never thought of.

Dreams have people dancing
Eating ice cream and sweets
Dreams have people frightened
Of running and falling
Through streets.

Some say that I'm a daydreamer
But really I'm just thinking of faraway places,
Blue seas and sandy beaches.

Dreams don't always come true
Although we like to think the nice ones do.
The dream that I like best
Is the one where I'm happy and greatly blessed.

Rachel Sharp (13)
St Augustine's School, Scarborough

The Dream Of All Dreams

Tonight I will have the dream of all dreams
The most marvellous dream I will ever have
And only when it is finished will I wake up.

In my dream there will be no war or fighting
And sweet bird songs will fill the air.

In my dream there will be no hungry people
Because everyone will have enough to eat.

In my dream there will be a place for everyone
To stay and to laugh over the happy times with
Their families.

In my dream there will be no bullying or racism
For each person, black and white, will live in
Peace and harmony with one another.

People share this dream across the globe,
But only when everyone in the world goes to
Sleep can this dream start.

Do you share this dream?

Juliet Foote (13)
St Augustine's School, Scarborough

Why?

Why do the government run around
After things that do not matter?
Why do some people die from hunger
While others get fatter and fatter?

Why do we bomb each other
When less soldiers get killed than civilians?
Why do people flee in terror
To fill camps which already hold millions?

Why do some die under the burning sun
As all their crops fail?
Why do some have thousands of tons of food
And if you take a little bit you'll be in jail?

Why are some tortured
When they haven't done anything?
Why is the guilty person running free and
Acting like a king?

Why can't this world live in peace?

Why?

Madeline Crosswaite (12)
Settle Middle School, Settle

In My World . . .

In my world . . .
No one is hungry
Because they live on dreams.
In my world . . .
No one is poor
Because stories are the universal currency.
In my world . . .
No one is sad
Because happiness is free.
In my world . . .
No one is lonely
Because everyone is a friend.
In my world . . .

Sophie Devlin (12)
Skipton Girls' High School, Skipton

The Dream Of A World

Throughout the world my dream is broken,
By the people, to which it is spoken,
And yet, to them it is of most use,
Breaking the ties of damage and abuse.

People living in poverty,
Without good sovereignty,
Suffering and hatred still,
Written into human will.

Independence from the strains,
Living in the starving lanes,
Africa and the same,
Cannot help the poor and lame.

All those things you take for granted,
Are the things they've always wanted.

Jacob Wilkins (13)
South Holderness Technology College, Preston

Wasted Dreams

My pillow like a feather,
The blanket warming like molten embers,
The gateway of my mind open,
Ready to embrace the light,
And shift me to my dream-ridden plight.

People shuffling in the brightness,
Animals relax in unearned luxury,
Machines labour without complaint,
Earning their distasteful keep,
The second-hand food forces them awake,
These servants give and give but never take.

Existence without meaning,
Instinct without survival,
We create the perfect servants,
To fuel our incessant needs,
They must bow down to me,
This is called slavery.

We banned it once,
Now it returns,
Their hard silver bodies,
Like the black men of old,
Now you find that people lied,
I shall stand and take their side.

I have a dream,
One where man and woman are partners,
We work together, play together,
Animals are our friends,
For life is but a gleam,
But I still have a dream,
Do you?

Peter Reynolds (14)
South Holderness Technology College, Preston

I Have A Dream!

I have a dream, no ordinary dream
Not full of swirls - 'n' twirls.
No!
It's a dream, a dream of hope,
Hope for life.
Hope for happiness.
Hope for friendship.
A dream to stop racism,
To stop war,
To stop murder,
To stop illness.
A dream to spread peace,
Peace between countries,
Peace between religions,
Peace between enemies.
A dream to love,
To love each other,
To love ourselves,
To love our planet.

Jessica Hitchcock (13)
South Holderness Technology College, Preston

World!

You can change the world
By the thoughtful things you do;
Making a difference
Letting our love shine through.

Reaching out to help others,
With the compassion we can give,
No matter who you are
No matter what you do
Or where you come from
We are all the same.

Bekki Norrison (13)
South Holderness Technology College, Preston

Young Writers - I Have A Dream Inspirations From Yorkshire

Have You Ever Thought?

Have any of you ever thought about how I may feel?
You all may laugh at me, giggle or grin,
But why can't you see I just want to fit in?
Yes.
You succeed in making me feel like a geek,
When you sit there chatting in your little clique,
To ever be picked to go in your team,
Well that to me is only a dream!

Have you ever thought about how you may treat me?
You all may tease me, spit or kick,
But have you ever realised that I'm not so thick?
No
But I won't be your punchbag anymore,
And, if you haven't realised, I no longer adore
You and your group of friends, as I am all I'll ever be,
And I guess that leaves you
To accept me as me.

Abbi Bainton (13)
South Holderness Technology College, Preston

The Dream

I dream of wealth crisp and cold,
I dream like Tithonus to never grow old.

I dream of loves wrong and right,
I dream of passions burning bright.

I dream of power to quell the masses,
I dream of servants filling wine glasses.

I dream of conquests throughout this land,
I dream to walk on golden sands.

I dream the dream of the human race . . .

. . . a vanity we must now face . . .

Peter Richard Stones (18)
South Holderness Technology College, Preston

I Have A Dream, I Want To Be Remembered

I want to be remembered
Doesn't need to be by many
Just one will do for me
To be a presence in their mind
On their memory, it need not be much.

I want to be remembered
Not just as a government number
A couple of dates marking my existence
A photograph dotted here and there
But as a real person, not merely data.

I want to be remembered
Not for launching a thousand ships
Or as a fair Greek pharaoh in equine milk
Nor as a ruler, man in soul, with feeble body
And not as the beauties painted in spring.

I want to be remembered
Words of inspiration
Actions aiding needy
Always being the last priority
Changing a life.

I don't want to be wept for
Or overly honoured
Just good memories
Of deeds remembered
That is my dream.

Katherine Brown (18)
South Holderness Technology College, Preston

If The World Was Backwards

If the world was backwards,
You and I would be black not white,
Our friends would be our enemies,
And our enemies would be our friends.

If the world was backwards,
The wealthy countries would have the famine,
And not the poor countries,
The poor countries would be the ones dictating to us,
And not the other way around.

If the world was backwards,
Those who are disabled
Would be free from their imprisonment,
Those who are different,
Would be the same as everyone else.

If the world was backwards,
Yesterday wouldn't be yesterday
Today wouldn't be today,
I wouldn't be me
And you wouldn't be you.

Don't change yourself for other people
Just be you
Cos
To the world you are one person,
But to one person you may be the world.

Hannah Broadley (14)
South Holderness Technology College, Preston

I Have A Dream

I have a dream,
An achievable dream,
Yet it is still to be achieved.

It is a dream deeply rooted in the bowels of the Earth,
Where it seeks release,
Yet the dream remains there still.

Repressed by human kind,
Held inside by greed,
Yet we have the power to set it free.

We are a parasite to our host,
No end to our destruction,
Yet there is still hope.

Hope for our salvation,
We hear not the words of Jesus,
Yet we preach them still.

Our abuse of our planet must stop,
We say that it will,
Yet it doesn't.

I have a dream,
I dream of an end to our devastating rage,
Yet it continues still,

Will the dream ever be made true?

Lewis Hodgson (14)
South Holderness Technology College, Preston

Tomorrow

I pray that tomorrow, no one will live in fear,
Free from conflict, harm and tear,
Poverty will be undone,
Famine, there will be none.

Every country shall unite,
Evil is what they'll smite,
And when it's destroyed, when it's done,
Equal rights for everyone!

Today is full of regret and sorrow,
I pray for a better tomorrow.

Matthew Copeman & George Christian (13)
South Holderness Technology College, Preston

Different

I am different but aren't you too?
You make me cry but what did I do?
The things you say, do you realise they hurt?
The pain you cause me, what is it worth?

All it takes is one smile to brighten my day,
A free gesture, nothing to pay.
Don't look at me strangely as if I'm a freak,
Why is it I'm afraid to speak?

Tall, short, fat and thin,
Black, white, many origins.
We are all different but need to learn,
We should judge from the inside to stop all the pain!

I have a dream so make it come true
Judge others like they should judge you.

Jessica Poole (14)
South Holderness Technology College, Preston

No More War!

No more fighting, no more war!
What exactly are you fighting for?
People die because of religion,
Wars are wrong, they aren't fun.
Friends, family, loved ones die,
People get hurt oh why, why, why?

Christian, Muslim, Jew, Hindu,
Why fight over religion when there's no need to?
We're all the same each and every day,
But religion always gets in the way.

The sound of explosions it scares me,
What I would give for peace and harmony!
Precious money wasted on weapons
Just to kill innocent citizens!

I hope you can see that wars kill
It's a terrible thing, not a thrill
Wars need to be stopped
So help us please to *stop, stop, stop!*

Danielle Agar (13) & Olivia Baker
South Holderness Technology College, Preston

I Have A Dream

I have a dream, I dream of innocent people dying
Women waiting for their loved ones to return
In this dream, starving children are crying
And for food, thousands do yearn.

I have a dream, but it's not a dream at all
It's a terrifying nightmare
Where diseases and illnesses over bodies do crawl
And food and water are incredibly rare.

I have a dream, and no matter how much I try to awake
It's still happening in the world today
All I want, for those pained people's sake
Is food, clean water, and a warm and safe place to lie.

I have a dream, though I want to dream no more
But how do I make it stop?
But it's not for my own sake, it's for the needy and the poor
Because for every day that goes by, their spirits drop.

I cannot do it alone, but the world can
Come together and unite, for your fellow man.

Rebecca Crawley (13)
South Holderness Technology College, Preston

I Have A Dream!

Most people wish for simple or insane things,
Like money or to fly with wings,
But me I have a dream,
As strange as it may seem.

This is my dream
No war but peace,
No hate but love,
No enemies but friends.

A world free from suffering and pain,
A world with no black or white,
A world of peace and calm,
A world that is all for love.

A world that is all for *you!*

Laura Wattam (14)
South Holderness Technology College, Preston

I Have A Dream

I have a big dream,
Of playing for United,
Playing with the best,
That includes Rooney and Giggs,
Van Nistelrooy too
The manager is Fergie,
And he is the greatest,
And that is my biggest dream.

I had a great dream,
That the world would be football,
Nothing would stop it,
Boys and girls can play,
Big adults can play,
Children would be taught by pros,
Nothing but the best,
And that is my greatest dream.

Thomas Baldwin (13)
Wingfield Comprehensive School, Rotherham

I Have A Dream . . .

I have a dream . . .
To stop child abuse and give children better lives.

I have a dream . . .
To help and care for people who need our love and care.

I have a dream . . .
To put a lid on racism.

I have a dream . . .
To influence people to do better in life.

I have a dream . . .
To make the world excellent not disgraceful

I have a dream . . .
To send a message out to all the poor, hungry victims
Giving food, money and love.

I have a dream . . .
To give a basket of joy to all the sad, unhappy, lonely people.

I have a dream.

Georgina Cutts (12)
Wingfield Comprehensive School, Rotherham

I Have A Dream!

I have a dream
That me and my mum
Go shopping all day
And I spend my mum's money away!

I get a new pair of shoes
Designed by Rebecca Loos
My mum gets some chocs
And I get my nan some socks!

My mum buys herself a dress
And I look in my mirror to see if my hair's a mess!
I get a pair of FCUK jeans
And my mum buys us a McD's.

Jade Reynolds (13)
Wingfield Comprehensive School, Rotherham

I Had A Dream

I wish I could play
Football in the sun all day
On the 13th of May

I would like to play
For Rotherham United
Then be an international
And when I'm older
I'd get rid of Sven
And become the manager
Lead England to victory
At the World Cup.

Then I will retire at 60 years old
And have a million bars of gold
I would buy the Playboy mansion
And party with the playgirls
Till I die.

Jake Phillips (12)
Wingfield Comprehensive School, Rotherham

If I Had A Dream

I had a dream
In my very own world
Everything was beautiful
But the weather, so cold.
Then all of a sudden, everything changed
I was stood on the stage
With the audience in range.
They cheered me on as I acted with a smile
I acted and acted, but only for a while.
Everything changed, I won an Oscar award
So proud I was that I tried so hard
Then suddenly I appeared back in my bed
'Man that was a cool dream,' I said.
I wonder what I'll dream tonight
Hopefully it won't give me a fright!

Jack Rowe (12)
Wingfield Comprehensive School, Rotherham

Kitten

I have a dream
A dream of a kitten
Playing in the sun
Climbing up the curtains
And sleeping all day long.

I have a dream
A tiny ginger kitten
A playful little kitten
A funny little kitten
An orange ball of fluff.

Adopting a kitty
From the animal sanctuary
Taking it home
In a little cardboard box
He now belongs to me.

Nicola Slazak (12)
Wingfield Comprehensive School, Rotherham

We Need To Stop Poverty

Let's stop poverty
No food
No water
No shelter
No electricity
No school
No life.

Let's stop poverty
Give them food
Give them water
Give them shelter
Give them electricity
Give them education
Give them life.

So let's stop poverty.

Mitchel Wright (12)
Wingfield Comprehensive School, Rotherham

I Had A Dream

I had a great dream
Of getting a Labrador
Rolling in the grass
Playing with all his big toys
In the gleaming sun
With his brunette fluffy fur
Barking with his friends
Cunning and chasing
Is my greatest dream.

Burying his bones
Digging and chewing
Is what he did do
Slurping all his sloppy food
He sat for treats
Dashed around with his ball
Jumped up at me
With one toy, ready to play
This is my best dream.

Aaron Green (12)
Wingfield Comprehensive School, Rotherham

I Have A Dream . . .

I have a dream to change the world!
Dream . . .
The third world out there
Dream . . .
Changing their lives
Dream . . .
Be the person to do that
Dream . . .
They don't have food
Dream . . .
They have a life but not like us!
Dream . . .
Be the person to be that dreamer . . .

Dale Goodwin (12)
Wingfield Comprehensive School, Rotherham

I Have A Dream

I had a dream that one year
All the expensive things wouldn't seem so dear
As I would be a millionaire
And could afford to travel anywhere.

I would live in a big house in Spain
And would have a well-known name
Everyone would look up at me
As I'd be the person they want to be.

With my money I wouldn't be tight
I would go shopping all day and night
I would give money to the poor
And poor they would be no more.

I'd try my best to keep the world safe
And make it a better place
I had a dream that one year
The world wouldn't be full of fear.

Charlotte Harwood (13)
Wingfield Comprehensive School, Rotherham

I Have A Dream . . .

Animals have feelings too,
Not just us.
Why do we feel we have the right,
To abuse and hurt them?
Imagine, do you like to be kicked, starved
And left in the street to die?
They don't ask for much,
Don't you see?
All they want is to be loved, to be
Cared for, to feel wanted.
If you love them, they'll love you back
So make a difference
Make them happy,
Please stop animal cruelty.

Paige Dow (12)
Wingfield Comprehensive School, Rotherham

I Have A Dream

I have a dream that
I could play for Liverpool
They are the best team
Steven Gerrard is the best
Player in the world
Liverpool will win the League
Because we're the best
We are better than the rest
That is my best dream.

Reds, Reds are the best
The ball will go in the net
In most of our games
We've got the best manager
Benitez is great
Running rings around teams
Running and kicking
And volleying too.
This is my best dream.

Waqar Majid (12)
Wingfield Comprehensive School, Rotherham

I Have A Dream

I have a dream that one day I can be
Someone whose dreams come true
By keeping my dream strong
Every single day of my life.
Someone who's known for the amazing things
That she has tried to do.
To change the different opinions of how people see of each other.
The way people separate themselves from others
Just because of the colour of their skin.
Maybe to change the world.
        Well, maybe half of the world!

Sinethemba Dumani (12)
Wingfield Comprehensive School, Rotherham

I Have A Dream!

I have a dream
I am very rich
I have a big house
And a football pitch.

I have a heart-shaped pool
And a heart-shaped island
Isn't that cool
Also, I have a house in Thailand.

I have my very own beach
I swim in the deep blue sea
I have a magic tree with apples, oranges and peaches
Everyone wants to be me.

The end of my dream is coming near
I'm starting to awake with a gleam
In my eye I have a little tear
Tonight I had a wonderful dream.

Natasha Bell (12)
Wingfield Comprehensive School, Rotherham

I Had A Dream

I had a dream
No one could stop me
I couldn't stop running
Running for my team.

Nine laps to go
But I was getting excited
While the crowd were delighted
My dream to win the gold medal
Was a success
As Great Britain won with me.

Danielle Jones (12)
Wingfield Comprehensive School, Rotherham

I Had A Dream!

I had a dream
Where I travelled to many places
In one place I saw a stream
When I looked I saw lots of faces.

Some looked happy, others looked sad
There were old ones, young and babies too,
The happy were good, the rest were bad
What was I to do?

Look! There was something
It was the sun shining down its rays,
All the faces began to sing,
And gave the sun lots of praises.

Now I know my time had come,
I woke up with a gleam,
I saw my mum,
And I knew it was the end of my wonderful dream.

Mariam Hassan (13)
Wingfield Comprehensive School, Rotherham

I Have A Dream

A dream that everyone has freedom of speech
A dream that a child's voice makes a big difference
A dream that every person or animal's right is respected
A dream that cruelty to animals is not tolerated
A dream that everyone will stand up for themselves
A dream that the water is clear and the air so fresh
A dream that every child has a smile on their face.

I had a dream that no one cared about anything . . .
It was a nightmare
That I hope will never come to reality.

Clarice Tejada (12)
Wingfield Comprehensive School, Rotherham

I Have A Dream

I have a dream
That just one day
Me and my sister would get on okay
We would not fight
Go shopping all night.

We would chill out by day
But that's okay.

Although we're not the best of friends
Our sisterly love will never end.

We would do each other's hair
We would not care
Whatever those jealous people may say.

I have a dream
That just one day
My sister and me would get on okay
That is all I dream each day.

Vicky Warrington (13)
Wingfield Comprehensive School, Rotherham

I Have A Dream . . .

I have a dream that one day poverty will be over.
I have a dream that war will be over someday
Because people are losing their lives.
I have a dream that racism will stop.
Imagine
That abuse will stop towards young children.
Imagine
That bullies will stop bullying people and calling them names.
Imagine
That drugs and violence will stop
Just think one day the world can come together as one.

Amy Gillott (12)
Wingfield Comprehensive School, Rotherham

I Have A Dream

I have a dream
My dream is here
I have to make it come true
The shelter, the food
We're here today
To keep them safe
And help them pray.

I have a dream
To keep them safe
Away from all the violence
Which could be silence.

We need to say
We go their way
To keep them warm
And calm.

We give them food
To help them live
Which everyone wants to do
They think of me like a star in their lives.

Rebekah Shortt (13)
Wingfield Comprehensive School, Rotherham

I Have A Dream . . . To Change The World

Imagine
AIDS being cured!
Imagine
People smiling!
Imagine
Disabled kids like me not being bullied!
Imagine
Bullying has stopped!
Imagine
Wars are over!
Imagine
No racism!
Imagine
No violence!
Imagine
Black and white people together!
Imagine
World peace!
Imagine
All the bad things in the world
Have stopped!

Leigh-Anne Jones (12)
Wingfield Comprehensive School, Rotherham

Dreams

I had a dream about
Flying through the air,
With the beautiful birds,
Climbing Mount Everest
In the dark, damp night.

I had a dream about
Being a top celebrity,
Winning loads of awards,
Playing my guitar on stage,
With the fabulous James Blunt.

I had a dream about
Living in a mansion
With loads of servants,
Having a movie star boyfriend,
With loads of cash.

I had a dream about
Having loads of setters.
I had to live in a massive house,
I stopped world hunger,
Everyone was happy.

I had a dream about
No school, no work,
Everyone loved it,
All I wanted in my life
Was a limo with a chauffeur.

I had a dream
Everyone lived for eternity
With no one to fear,
If you wished upon a star,
Your wonderful dreams would come true.

I had a dream.

Laura Tompkins (11)
Wingfield Comprehensive School, Rotherham

I Have A Dream

I have a dream that I wish one day
We can stop wars
When we have to drink
And smash the bottles in bars
Live in a nation where
People will not be judged by the colour of their skin
When your dreams come true
You will win
No dreamer is
Ever too small
No dream ever too big
Or too tall
As the children to have fun
But I am standing next to the burning sun
As the day goes on when it goes again
When the war has been done it comes
To an end.

Marcus Senior (12)
Wingfield Comprehensive School, Rotherham

I Had A Dream

I have a dream where anyone can dare to be different.
Where people are not judged by the way they dress
Or their choice of piercing.
I have a dream, where people who believe in freedom of speech
Do not just disappear.
Where a corrupt politician will not rule the world.

I have a dream where a woman will not fear the man
That is supposed to love her.
When the key turns in the lock she flinches like she feels a sharp pain.
I had a dream,
It was broken.

Phoebe Trezise (12)
Wingfield Comprehensive School, Rotherham

I Have A Dream

I have a dream
That Rotherham United will get promoted
I have a dream
That one day I will go to Wembley with my family
I have a dream!

I have a dream
That my loving family will live forever and ever
I have a dream
For everybody to live happily with a roof over their head
I have a dream!

I have a dream
That there are no bullies around anyone
I have a dream
That nobody gets punished for something they didn't do
I have a dream!

I have a dream
That poverty goes away forever
I have a dream
For everyone to have their say in discussions
I have a dream.

Jack Wright (12)
Wingfield Comprehensive School, Rotherham

I Have A Dream . . .

Think
Put an end to racism
Think
Make voices be heard
Think
As a gift to those who aren't as wealthy
Hand over food
Think
Put a light at the end of that
Dark, gloomy tunnel
Think
Inspire people, make things better for those
Listening ears.
Think
Stamp a full stop on bullying and animal cruelty,
Make the people pay who abuse children.
Think
Speak out loud, don't be one of the silent crowds
Think
Make your actions speak louder than your words
Think
Change the future, make it better
Don't make it worse.

Be happy!

Harriet Cliff (12)
Winqfield Comprehensive School, Rotherham

I Have A Dream

I have a dream . . .
To let the world work as one
I have a dream . . .
That nobody will be alone
I have a dream . . .
To be accepted, black or white
I have a dream . . .
To be the light in people's lives
I have a dream . . .
For peace throughout the world
I have a dream . . .
That insults will not be hurled
I have a dream . . .
For love to be spread
I have a dream . . .
For kind words to be said
I have a dream . . .
For no one to be poor
I have a dream . . .
For people's minds not to be sore
I have a dream . . .
To wander far
I have a dream . . .
To be accepted for who you are.

Robyn Brookes (11)
Wingfield Comprehensive School, Rotherham

I Have A Dream

I have a dream where that girl has a voice,
I have a dream where that girl is listened to,
Where that girl has a say,
I have a dream where that girl can say 'No'
Where that girl can say 'Stop!'

I have a dream where that girl has a mind,
I have a dream where that girl can make choices,
Where that girl can think about things,
I have a dream where that girl can like people,
Where that girl can speak her mind.

I have a dream where that girl has a body,
I have a dream where that girl isn't spat at,
Where that girl isn't bullied,
I have a dream where that girl can join in games,
Where that girl can walk proud.

I have a dream where that girl has a heart,
I have a dream where that girl can be loved,
Where that girl has feelings,
I have a dream where that girl has friends,
Where that girl has a family.

I have a dream where I am no longer
        'That Girl'.

Chloe Bennett (12)
Wingfield Comprehensive School, Rotherham

I Have A Dream . . .

To bake a cake
Full of love
To bake a cake
Crammed with trust
With mixed in support
To bake a cake
With added beauty
And with my cake I will conquer poverty
Conquer hate
My cake is my dream
And my cake
Is pure
It's sprinkled with kindness
And decorated with ongoing spirit
My cake is my dream
And one day this dream
Will come true.

Madelaine Houghton (12)
Wingfield Comprehensive School, Rotherham

I Have A Dream

I have a dream
To be a footballer
Where the crowd go wild
And chant my name.

I have a dream
To make world peace
So everyone is friends
And no one has wars.

I have a dream
To make the world safer
Put all the thugs in prison
So people can go out not afraid.

Jamie Hensman (13)
Wingfield Comprehensive School, Rotherham

I Have A Dream

I have a dream
The weather is bad
War is at risk
I nearly lose Dad.

But he comes home
I am so glad
I give him a hug
I love my dad.

My family are here
For when I come home
With my family and friends
I'm never alone.

I stood on a tower
And looked over the land
The wind on my face
So warm by the hand.

Then came peace
All over, no fear
Everyone smiled
No more tears.

I wished for clouds
So fluffy and white
And in the fog clearing
I saw a light.

A puppy appeared
I threw the ball
My friends by my side
Are there when I fall . . .

Emma Woodland (12)
Wingfield Comprehensive School, Rotherham

I Have A Dream

I wish everyone was equal
I wish everyone wasn't racist

You wish something could change
Deep down in your heart
Everyone is loved
Everyone is the same
Nobody would fight
I wish the world was in peace
Everyone wasn't judged by colour
Only by characters.

Actions speak louder than words
Please don't regret it
A dream fills you with love and care
No dreamer is to big for their dreams
One chance to change the world
Would you take it or not?

Please follow your dreams
They might come true.

Adam Purshouse (11)
Wingfield Comprehensive School, Rotherham

I Have A Dream

I have a dream that my community
Will not suffer violence
That people can learn to get along.
I have a dream that people don't use weapons
To resolve situations
And that we can live in safety.

I have a dream that I can live in my home without fear
That in my home I will never be afraid.
I have a dream that I can sleep
Without the thought of being robbed
And that I won't have to worry again.

I have a dream that my family will not be harmed
That they can live in peace.
I have a dream that my sister will never have to cry in fear
And that she'll always be safe.

I have a dream that my parents will never fight again
That my parents won't suffer pain.
I have a dream that small children won't see abuse or violence
And that they won't be abused themselves.

Ryan Bates (13)
Wingfield Comprehensive School, Rotherham

I Had A Dream

I had a dream
All pleasant and calm
That Rotherham United won the Cup
And Liverpool beat Man U.
I had a dream that
Nobody could tell me
What to do
Or where to go.
I had a dream that hearts
Could fly instead of birds.

I had a dream that
School was banned
And we could do
What we wanted
When we wanted.
We ate ice cream and chocolate cake
But then I woke up.

Jade Dixon (11)
Wingfield Comprehensive School, Rotherham

What A World That Would Be

I have a dream of a brand new world where everyone is the same,
And laws and rules existed
And evil was very distant
What a world that would be.

A new world with no poverty, AIDS or cancer,
No racism or murderers at all
And no one with any bombs
And wars don't exist
What a world that would be.

When you can follow your heart
To where your dreams will start
And think what a world that would be.

Kieran Bartholomew (12)
Wingfield Comprehensive School, Rotherham

I Had A Dream

I had a dream, the world was great!
No fighting, no war, just love and happiness.
Everyone glad to be alive!
Children playing on the sunny streets.
Laughter round each corner.

I had a dream, I saw fear!
People wishing they lived somewhere else.
War round every corner, terror!
Black clouds, the sun hiding away,
Screams, bombs dropping from the skies!

I woke up thinking about the dream!
Realising that my last dream was . . .
Similar to the world we live in today!
How much I wish the world was
Just like dream one!

Bethany Cudworth (12)
Wingfield Comprehensive School, Rotherham

A Dream!

I have a dream
To live in a society
Without . . .

Litter, litter, spreading around
The town,
Litter, litter, attracting insects
On the ground.

Litter, litter is so foul
It will make you want to run a mile.

Without litter, litter, the town would be so clean
It would be like a washing machine.

Martin Harwood (13)
Wingfield Comprehensive School, Rotherham

Dream Of A Dream

I had a dream,
About a dream.
Full of peace and love,
Wondering what it's like up above.
I had a dream,
About what it would be like to be
Someone else unlike me.
I wish I could look more unique,
So I wouldn't be judged.
I had a fantasy,
About a new world,
A new me.
In that world,
Everything and everyone felt equal.
Rich helped the poor,
There was no such thing as war,
And people could have more and more.
People lived life to the full,
Not die and the world remain dull.

I drifted away
Imagining everyone had the best health,
I fell asleep,
Dreaming that I had fame and fortune
But the dream I want to be true,
Is for me to be the luckiest girl
In the entire world.

Nicola Howdle (12)
Wingfield Comprehensive School, Rotherham

I Have A Dream

I have a dream,
Where I will be spoilt,
By fussy grandparents spending all their money on me,
They would buy me treasures
Only the best for me!

My mother would cook me a banquet for tea
She would wait on me, hand and foot,
My sister is my slave,
To do everything I tell her.
Only the best for me.

A room just for my chocolate
A house just for myself,
A plasma TV in every room
And all of the best channels,
Only the best for me!

My clothes are all designer
My shoes are custom made
When I say, 'Mum can I have this?'
She says, 'OK.'
Only the best for me!

I'd have everything I want,
I'd do anything I want,
I'd wear anything I want,
And I'd behave how I want.
Only a dream for me!

Luke Powell (13)
Wingfield Comprehensive School, Rotherham

I Have A Dream!

I have a dream
Where there's no divorce
Nor funeral carriage
Nor widow alone
To bear the pain
Not a burning tear
To drop from the eye.

No cancer to wave
Goodbye, goodbye.

But where my family
Will be stood
Waiting for me . . .
To belong where I will
With open arms
Ready to say
'Welcome home love'
I dreamt this day.

Rebekah Wilkinson (12)
Wingfield Comprehensive School, Rotherham

I Have A Dream

Fun,
I dream that everyone can have it
Health,
I dream no one lives without it
Family,
I dream everyone has one
Mates,
I dream everyone can trust someone.

Fear,
I dream no one should feel it
Fights,
I dream that no one should have to start one
Grudge,
I dream no one holds one
War,
I dream it never existed.

I dream that everyone feels the same.

Shannon Wheeler (13)
Wingfield Comprehensive School, Rotherham

I Have A Dream . . .

I have a dream,
I sense my future is good,
I feel more alive,
Every single day,
I am yet to show what I can give,
Doctors are lifesavers,
I want the world to have peace,
In which they will be happy.

Give people chances
Even if they do wrong,
Everyone deserves a second chance,
Let them start fresh,
The world should be safer,
As you get older,
It should be filled with joy and laughter,
Not crime and dullness.

The world should not fight,
We could help each other in many ways,
It may take a while,
But we are here to do right,
Have jobs and live life properly,
The heart of people's family may be broken,
In fact it may be stolen,
If - they - died.

Phillip Pinder (13)
Wingfield Comprehensive School, Rotherham

I Have A Dream

I have a dream where no one suffers,
From diseases that can kill.
That no one can ever die,
No one deserves to be dead and still.

I have a dream where all violence stops,
To adults, animals and children.
Also, no one lives on the streets,
They have a family with them.

I have a dream, I have a dream,
Where I can be a star.
I have a dream, I have a dream,
That I can travel afar.

I have a dream, I have a dream,
Where there are no wars,
I have a dream, I have a dream,
Where everybody is a star.

I have dreams,
You have dreams,
He has dreams,
She has dreams,
They have dreams,
We have dreams,
And hopefully they will come true.

Kimberley Edwards (13)
Wingfield Comprehensive School, Rotherham

Aspirations

I have a dream,
That people will love fellow humans,
Not because they have money,
But for who that person is.

I have a dream,
That every bully must be prosecuted,
For they are insensitive, ignorant and imbeciles,
Nobody should have the pain . . . nobody.

I have a dream,
That Manchester United will win a cup,
However big it may be.
Rotherham United will win the Premiership,
What a dream that would be!

Last, but not least,
I have a dream,
That I will become the world's biggest selling artist,
Bigger than any other.
This was my dream, these were my dreams.

William Burrows (13)
Wingfield Comprehensive School, Rotherham

I Have A Dream

I have a dream
All illnesses will be cured
The fear of losing a loved one will vanish
That is my dream.

I have a dream
Nothing should suffer
Everyone will be treated the same
That is my dream.

I have a dream
No one should sit and wait for death to creep upon them
Everyone will look on the bright side
That is my dream.

I have a dream
Dying should not be an option
Treasure every day as life flies
That is my dream.

> I have a dream
> Do you?

Sarah Coult (13)
Wingfield Comprehensive School, Rotherham

I Have A Dream

I have a dream
To be the best that I can be
The hungry will be fed
To end the poverty.

I have a dream
For people to be happy
When problems come their way
They'll sort them out real snappy.

I have a dream
To help people at every age
Everyone will be treated fairly
And get a decent wage.

I have a dream
To accomplish all these things
But many more dreams will come to me
To spread the wind beneath my wings.

Amy Adams (13)
Wingfield Comprehensive School, Rotherham

I Had A Dream

School!
I had a dream that everyone was good and nobody got told off.
I had a dream that school was fun, more fun
Than having holidays and I always wanted to go every day
And never go home.
I had a dream that we did not work at all,
Just played games and talked to anyone we liked.
I had a dream and it was real, I was there.

Leanne Sanderson (11)
Wingfield Comprehensive School, Rotherham

I Have A Dream

I have a dream,
That all children should have a loving family and every single being
Should be loved.
I have a dream,
That no child should not hear the people they love being abused or
                                                    getting hurt.

I have a dream,
That everybody should have a chance to live their life without anyone
Or anything getting in their way and stopping it.
I have a dream,
That every child on Earth deserves a right to education,
No matter how rich or how poor.
I have a dream,
That people will not be judged by the colour of their skin or hair,
But should be judged by their character and personality.
I have a dream,
That people like Martin Luther King should be respected and not
Treated like a criminal.
People like this can help to change this world and to make dreams
                                                    come true.
One day you'll feel like Ellen MacArthur and you will have to face the
World on your own.
When people feel alone they need to understand that at least
A thousand other people are feeling equally the same.
Ellen felt like she had a team behind her, supporting her.
Remember, whenever you feel alone, think of how many people you
Could look up to
How many people could make you feel safe.
Never cry or frown because you never know who is falling in love
With your smile.
I have a dream,
That everybody should have a dream.

Lucy Brookes (13)
Wingfield Comprehensive School, Rotherham

I Have A Dream

I have a dream
That my family will not quarrel
So that there will be no heartache
It makes you really sad, you don't want to be at home
You want to spend your time alone.

I have a dream
That people want to share
To share it is really nice
It makes people feel happy inside
So that's why I wish people would share it
Shows that you really care.

I have a dream
That people will not commit crime
It makes you feel unsafe inside
It makes people want to run and hide
So I say stop it now or you might do something you regret.

Chris Winsor (13)
Wingfield Comprehensive School, Rotherham

I Had A Dream

I had a dream that I could fly
I had a dream that I could sing
I had a dream that I could fly to space and back
I had a dream that I could be a shark
I had a dream that I could fly an aeroplane in the sky
I had a dream that was rich
I had a dream that I could touch the northern lights
I had a dream that I could climb the highest mountain
I had a dream that I could be eaten by a clown
I had a dream that I could be a worm
I had a dream that I could be eaten by a bird.

Daniel Adams (12)
Wingfield Comprehensive School, Rotherham

A Dream

I have a dream.

I have a dream,
A dream to support animals in need,
To support poorly animals,
Can it happen?
Yes it can!

I have a dream

I have a dream,
A dream to go round town and not see anyone
Anyone scrounging for money.
Can it happen?
Yes it can!

I have a dream

I have a dream,
A dream to play football for Leeds,
With the money I earn I could give my parents what they give me,
Can it happen?
Yes it can!

I have a dream

I have a dream
A dream to be a footballer,
I would go to schools and help kids achieve what I have.
Can it happen?
Yes it can!

I have a dream
A dream to get my dreams.

Can it all happen?
Yes! Yes!

Anything can happen in a dream.

I have a dream, what's yours?

Tom Heap (12)
Wingfield Comprehensive School, Rotherham

My Dream

I have a dream,
To run and represent Great Britain,
To bring gold medals back to our country,
And share my success with all those who support me.

Why does competition have to cause arguments?
Why do competitions have to cause wars?
Why do wars have to cause deaths?
Why do people's lives have to end?

The reason why competition has caused arguments has not
                                                been solved,

This is what I want.
This is what I want,
Is it possible for this to be solved, or will it stay this way forever?

There are still questions unsolved,
Will they be answered
Or is that just a joke?
Is it?

I have a dream,
But will it ever come true?
I have a dream,
I have a dream.

Ryan Broadhead (13)
Wingfield Comprehensive School, Rotherham

I Have A Dream . . .

I have a dream
That I shall not forget
Everyone gets a say
Not just the people in charge.

We will be free
Unless we've done wrong
No harm will be committed
To anything or anyone.

The ones who should die though
Are be the killers
To show what they do
To their unwilling victims.

All countries are united
So there will be no wars
And loved ones don't have to die for us
Unless aliens come.

That is my dream
I hope you'll remember it too
And I will now dream
That my dream will come true.

William Humphries (13)
Wingfield Comprehensive School, Rotherham

A Dream!

I have a dream to live in a better world
To have freedom, love, care
And soul down our hearts.
To have good loving people
And love one another
Just like God said.

How can we make our world a better place?

I have a dream to live in a world
Without smoking, any bullies or punishment
That is when people are behaving
And there's no animal abuse
Animals should be loved
Just like loving a human being.

What do you think?

I have a dream for everyone to live forever
For them not to die just like my auntie
People love one another
They don't want to lose each other.

What is our world like?

How can we change it?

I have a dream for our world
To have peace and love
Everyone to make the world a calm, peaceful world.

That is my dream
I do have a dream.

Judith Khumalo (12)
Wingfield Comprehensive School, Rotherham

Complete My Dreams

I have a dream that in the future . . .
I can fly through my ambitions
And complete my missions
Fight through my worries
With no hurries
Fly through time with no rush
Complete my problems like a big great crush
And complete with no rush
Sweep away when people dare to cross me
Flow past the wrong and stay on the right
And complete with no fright
Work through my problems with no hurry
While I try not to worry
And complete with no hurry.

Help people as they pass through difficult times
When they're experienced great problems or even crimes
And complete the future through good and bad times
Make people face right and wrong
Even if they stay in jail very long
And complete through on what they've done wrong
Gather their fears
Without any tears
And complete with no fears.

As the time goes by
My ambitions will continue to fly high.
And complete as the time goes by.

Elisabeth Kamaris (12)
Wingfield Comprehensive School, Rotherham

I Have A Dream

I have a dream
That world peace will happen, however
Would that restore order in the world?

I have a dream
That order should be restored in the world
But how should this be done, world peace?

I have a dream
That there is no war in the world
Consequently will this create world peace?

I have a dream
That people can walk about proud of themselves
Whether they be homosexual, black or speak a different tongue
They should not be judged.

But I leave by saying this

I had a dream
The answer to life, universe and everything.

Was I glad?
Discover for yourself in the journey of life, universe
And everything.

Thomas Alderson (12)
Wingfield Comprehensive School, Rotherham

A Better World

People have a right to speak their minds, without people laughing
And throwing it back in their face.

People have a right to be them; everyone is unique,
Instead of being a 'wanna be' and acting like someone else.

Think how much better our world would be.

Having a relationship with someone, that's strong and loyal,
With no secrets or lies.

No arguments that put people down, just conversations with a
Hint of happiness.

Think how much better our world would be.

Pure ambition to reach your goals, and successfully achieving them.

Building new goals when the rest are achieved, to set yourself
A higher ambition.

Think how much better our world would be.

No fear for people walking down the street in the dark,
With no one around, or fear of going down a snicket.

No fear for children of being kidnapped and held as prisoners.

Think how much better our world would be.

These are just a few of my dreams, but together we can dream
Many more.

Chloe Sanders (13)
Wingfield Comprehensive School, Rotherham

I Have A Dream!

I have a dream,
A dream to support animals in need,
Poorly animals.
Can it happen?
Yes it can.

I have a dream,
A dream to help the world,
To make the world a better world.
Can it happen?
I don't know to be honest.

I have a dream,
To become a footballer
So I can be rich,
But also, if I am rich, I can help animals
Can it happen?
Yes it can.

I have a dream,
A dream to have no thefts,
I hate thefts,
Can I get rid of them?
I don't know to be honest.

Jade Haffner (12)
Wingfield Comprehensive School, Rotherham

I Have A Dream!

I have a dream,
Do you?
I dream for many things . . .

One thing's for sure
I dream for no violence
Do you?

I dream children can be happy
Have safe homes
Do you?

People could help!
But how?
Do you know?

Children shouldn't get kicked
Even thrown down the stairs
Do you think?

They should be happy
Be warm, smile!
Are you?

I can answer that question,
Can you?

Jade Herbert (12)
Wingfield Comprehensive School, Rotherham

I Have A Dream

I have a dream that I can get rid of all the fossil fuels to make
It a cleaner place.
Do you?
I have a dream that I have loads of money.
Do you?
I have a dream that I can make the pollution go away.
Do you?
I have a dream that I have a really posh house.
Do you?
I have a dream that all the thugs will just disappear.
Do you?
I have a dream that I can own loads of football clubs.
Do you?
I have a dream that all the criminals are in jail.
Do you?
I have a big, big dream that everybody is happy and
everybody gets along.

      Do you?

Joe Hattersley (13)
Wingfield Comprehensive School, Rotherham

I Have A Dream!

I dream that children never have to cry about violence.
I dream that children feel safe in their home and environment.
I dream that when children get older they have good memories
About their childhood.
I dream that children have happy and enjoyable lives.
I dream that there are more safe houses where children go to
And tell people their problems.

Jannat Suleman (13)
Wingfield Comprehensive School, Rotherham

Peace In The World

I have a dream
To be a god, and make the world a better place,
For all the humans,
And the animals who
Sit and walk the streets at night.

Let the weather shine and gleam,
With no rain and no snow,
But maybe just at Christmas time.

For all crimes to stop and the people
Who have done them to go to jail,
For guns to be banned
And murder never to happen.

Animals run free and all zoos closed,
Hunting stopped for everyone
And the killing spree of animals decreased.

Mark Gleadall (13)
Wingfield Comprehensive School, Rotherham

I Had A Dream

I had a dream
A pleasant dream
About a pony
Named Leoney
She was big but,
Also tall
She could jump
As high as a tree trunk
Once she lent over
And ate a clover
Which made her get over excited
But she still made me delighted
Now I've woken up
I might get good luck.

Paris Watts (12)
Wingfield Comprehensive School, Rotherham

I Have A Dream!

I had a dream
My head up high
My body floating in the sky
It felt quite sad
It made me mad
To see all those fights
Are nearly every night
That's bullying I thought inside my head
When people are bullied they end up dead.

My dream is changing into something nice
Everywhere I look there's sweets and spice
I'm rich now
I wonder how
That's all I want, lots of money
Won't that be funny
I've got a pool and I'm having a party.

My dream won't last
It's drifting very fast
I'm laying awake in my bed
All those thoughts in my head.

Laura Hirst (13)
Wingfield Comprehensive School, Rotherham

What A Dreamer . . .

I have a dream
To become famous
To help the world
And all things in it.

I want to be rich
And live where the weather is hot
To be around the people I care for
And those who love me back.

I want to marry a footballer
Who will care for me.
I'd like to be a lady of leisure
To do the things I want to do.

I want all animals
To run free and wild,
For all hunting to be stopped
And all zoos closed.

I have a dream
That all crime is stopped,
And people who have done them should go to jail,
And murder never to happen.

Rebecca Foster (13)
Wingfield Comprehensive School, Rotherham

Dreams!

I have a dream,
Where there are no wars
So people feel safe
Safe to walk alone

I want a family
A family who loves
Who cares for one another
A family with their own dreams.

I have a dream
Where I have a job as an actress
An actress who people love and envy.

I want to see animals free
Free of chemicals
Abuse
And shame.

I want a house paid for
No expense
Rent free

I want to be free!

Samantha Dowell (12)
Wingfield Comprehensive School, Rotherham

I Have A Dream . . .

I have a dream
To live abroad
In a villa near the
Canary Islands.
Do you have a dream?
I dream of having a
Swimming pool and jacuzzi
In my back garden.

I hope it's going to be hot
I have a dream of sponsoring
Poor little children in Africa
And putting them in a very
Special children's home.

I need money to live on holiday,
I need a job to live on holiday,
Do you have a dream?
I have a dream of being a model to get money,
But that will never happen.

But I must remember it's
Only a dream.

Tara Davis (13)
Wingfield Comprehensive School, Rotherham

I Have A Dream . . .

I have a dream
To live in a warm country
Where the sun shimmers
Day after day.

To have a smashing job!
Which involves a lot of money
To lay on the beach
In the gleaming sun
But it's only a dream!

All the poor children in Africa
I want to help their lives extend
By giving them gifts and money
What would you do to help others?

When I'm older
Now you know how I want to live
But I must remember
It's only a dream!

Sophie Pritchard (12)
Wingfield Comprehensive School, Rotherham

Dream Of A Better World

I dream the end of racism and poverty
The Muslims happy with what they see
The Africans standing up healthy
And having plenty to eat for generations on end.

I dream the world without pollution and endless litter,
No more deadly diseases from the rubbish on the streets
And the percentage of people dying from pollution
Each year reduced.

I dream the world with reduced tax payments
To keep people warm with full stomachs
With hope of getting an education
And later on a job.

I dream the world without people that are cruel to animals
Zoos closed, animals free and less damaged animals
No need for a vet.

I dream the world with more forests
And something to write on
Without having to cut trees down.

> I dream a better world.

Zach Costello (12)
Wingfield Comprehensive School, Rotherham

I Have A Dream . . .

I have a dream to stop animal cruelty.
For people to stop abandoning dogs on the street
And abandoning other animals in the middle of nowhere.
This usually happens because their owners get fed up of them
Or they get too old!

Animals don't ask for much, they only ask for love and compassion
Animals should know that someone is there for them when no one

else is.

They want to be loved, not abandoned and abused!

Change the life of animals
Home and comfort them
Is that too much?

Imagine how you would feel if you were an animal,
Being abused then abandoned as soon as you got old.

Change the world and stop animal cruelty!

Shelbey Burton (12)
Wingfield Comprehensive School, Rotherham

My Dreams

I dream of being a famous scientist
Known across the world
I wish to see the world in all its glory
I dream of seeing a million sunsets
I wish to walk below the stars
And look up to a pollution-less sky
I dream of seeing the world dancing
I wish to see everyone smile
I dream of a world where we are not afraid to say what we have,
Not what we don't have
I wish to be judged by personality, not appearance
I dream of grasping a moment of happiness,
And never letting go
I wish for a place where dreams are made reality.

The world is a nightmare,
Let's make it a dream.

Laura Gillott (12)
Wingfield Comprehensive School, Rotherham